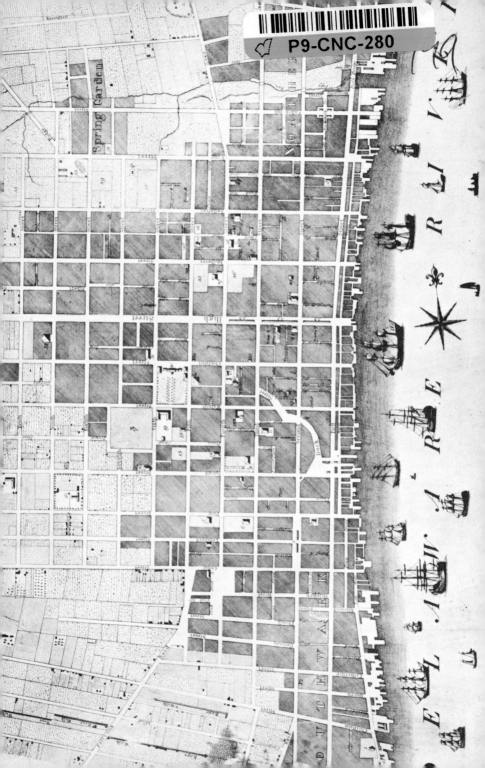

# VERDICT

# FOR

# THE DOCTOR

# Verdict for the Doctor

*The Case of Benjamin Rush*

BY

Winthrop & Frances Neilson

HASTINGS HOUSE, PUBLISHERS, NEW YORK

TO DOCTORS OF MEDICINE

*—And to Their Wives with Them*

Published simultaneously in Canada
by S. J. Reginald Saunders, Publishers, Toronto 2B.

Library of Congress Catalog Card Number: 58-9241

*Printed in the United States of America*

# Authors' Note

THIS BOOK is a profile in history. It is about an event: the men it concerned, and what took place.

The event is a trial, after an action brought by Dr. Benjamin Rush of Philadelphia, world-famous physician and signer of the Declaration of Independence, against William Cobbett, newspaperman who called himself "Peter Porcupine." The trial took place before the Supreme Court of Pennsylvania in the December term, 1799. The cause: slander.

Behind those bare facts of the trial lies a remarkable and incredible story. Benjamin Rush has long been remembered as a spectacular figure of the Revolution and one of our early outstanding doctors. But William Cobbett, the young Englishman who came to Philadelphia and nearly succeeded in turning us British again, has been too much forgotten.

Cobbett is still a hero in his native England as a Radical and champion of the people, a successor to John Wilkes and leader against the despotism of monarchy. Yet in earlier American days he was politically on the opposite side: with Alexander Hamilton an arch-conservative, a defender of George III, and savage opponent of Jefferson's principles of democracy.

Dr. Benjamin Rush, of an already old Philadelphia family, conservative and meticulous himself, was on the other hand a rebel in medicine, an advocate of progress, a democrat and life-long friend of Thomas Jefferson.

How the physician and the journalist came into their struggle-to-the-finish conflict is the story of this book.

We wish to thank Miss D. E. Collins in England as well as Hodder & Stoughton Ltd., publishers, for their permission to use Mr. G. K. Chesterton's wonderful description of Cobbett from his book *William Cobbett*.

*"He aimed well."*
—RUSH, *on Rush*

ᘐ

"The time of my writing will be looked back to as a memorable epoch, not only in American politics, but in the political mind of America."

—COBBETT, *on Cobbett*

ᘐ

# Contents

# List of Illustrations

# The Doctor

# 1

## *It Began on Friday, the 13th . . .*

T HE doctor's carriage rolled through Philadelphia's streets, along Spruce and then up Sixth toward Chestnut. He urged on the horse's fast pace, for he was late. People turned their heads at the sound of spinning wheels and clopping hoofbeats echoing over the paving stones and between the brick house fronts. They saw a man sitting intent, erect, with his high-crowned felt hat pulled forward slightly and the collar of his greatcoat fitting close around the back of his neck in protection against the cold.

He was a man of fifty-three, taller than average, slender, and his forehead was high as well as broad. A stubborn chin underscored his narrow, tapering face. His glance was sharp and alert, every move quick, decisive. His gloved hands held a nervous grip on the reins.

Most Philadelphians recognized him at once to be Dr. Benjamin Rush.

Some could shudder, remembering the same clattering of the doctor's urgent wheels in earlier years.

They guessed where he was driving now with such preoccupation. On this Friday morning, December 13, 1799, the doctor's libel case against the English newspaper writer was coming to trial. Gathering even at this moment in the celebrated State House were the jury and witnesses, spectators, and judges of the Supreme Court of Pennsylvania.

Philadelphia gossip made the trial the current topic of conversation. Yet few people not directly concerned with the case could comprehend the issues. The public saw a melodramatic clash between the world-famous doctor and the impassioned newspaperman, William Cobbett. The collision of personalities they could understand. Philadelphians had suffered and died through the times that produced the quarrel. Most citizens, on one side or the other, had been drawn into it.

The people did not know—at least on this morning the trial began—the precedents of law that must be established. They could not see that the essence of this lawsuit would stay alive for the predictable future of America.

Philadelphians thought of the new century ahead. The magic milestone date of 1800 was half a month away. An era was closing.

By curious coincidence, the decade ending was almost exactly bracketed by the deaths of Benjamin Franklin on April 17, 1790, and of George Washington on December 14, 1799. For these ten years Philadelphia, capital of the nation, had been a red-hot crucible tempering the steel of the new United States. It was a shakedown period. The two-party political system had emerged, a presidential election named Washington's successor. These were years of French Revolution, foreign intrigues, Alien and Sedition laws, the X Y Z Affair. It had been a decade of bitterest kinds of personal controversies, leading off with Hamilton

4

and Jefferson, when political differences grew into feuds that made enemies of neighbors. In the Quaker city of brotherly love, this was an age of vituperation, slanders, libels, half-truths flaunted in newspapers, and virulent verbal campaigns.

Controversy forged the nation's character. The decade proved an axiom that history is made by people, not by things.

Out of the maelstrom sprung one of the strangest trials ever to come before an American court. One of its lawyers called it the most important case ever presented to a jury. The causes were national. But the quarrel between a Philadelphia physician and the newspaperman who styled himself Peter Porcupine had turned for both men into an all-out battle for personal survival.

For a December day in Philadelphia, the weather was damp but fair. So far the winter had been open and mild, not like last year when by mid-December snowfalls had been especially heavy. It was to be Philadelphia's last year as the capital of the United States if, as expected, the new city of Washington would be ready to receive the Federal government. The five newspapers of the city carried news of the wars abroad and of the skirmishes involving American ships at sea, along with such local announcements as the evening performance of Rickett's Circus, doors to open at six with the show beginning precisely at seven. An ad gave notice that Thomas Dobson at the Stone-House, 41 South Second Street, was publishing a book by Benjamin Rush called *Observations on the Origin of the Malignant Bilious or Yellow Fever in Philadelphia*—price ³⁄₁₅ths of a dollar.

President John Adams was in town with Mrs. Adams. Congress was in session, the House meeting in Congress

5

Hall on Chestnut Street while the Senate sat in the State House, in the former courtroom to the right of the entrance door.

On the morning of the trial Dr. Rush was later than he meant to be. He had already been through his early rounds at the Pennsylvania Hospital. He was worried. Even his own lawyers offered little hope of victory in the lawsuit. Defeat would spell final ruin and justify his opponent's claims. Let the lawyers express interest in the legal precedents of freedom of the press. The jury's decision had infinite meaning for the nation, the doctor realized.

But the issue for him was a physician's right to practice his own system of medicine. Benjamin Rush could understand better than anyone else the importance of this trial to the entire medical profession. Future medical controversies were to be affected by what happened in this case. If new methods of treatment could never in all sincerity be tried, then progress in the science of medicine must forever stop.

As his wife Julia said, the outcome lay with the will of God.

Rush's face set grimly as he passed Congress Hall and approached the State House. The whole square outside the building was more crowded than usual. Sessions of the Senate and House of Representatives always brought out numbers of people, but the increase today could be attributed only to curiosity for one event—the Rush-Cobbett case.

The doctor frowned uneasily.

As he pulled to a halt, Peter, Dr. Rush's seventeen-year-old Negro serving boy, ran out to take his horse.

"Mis' Rush already in the court, sir," the boy said. "Miss Mary, she walked over from the house with her. They met Mr. Richard here."

6

"Very well, Peter."

The doctor stepped down from the carriage, conscious of the crowds. He heard the whisperings. He smoothed his cravat and pulled his coat straight.

"I wish you success, sir," Peter said.

Rush glanced at the earnest face of the boy. He was fond of Peter. He remembered the faithfulness of the little Negro, then eleven, in the yellow fever of 1793. Peter had been one of the few able to stand by him through the whole violent epidemic.

In a change of mood, the doctor grinned. "We will be successful for sure, Peter."

Then with all the confidence he could assume he crossed the pavement, entered the door, and went to the courtroom.

He had played other parts in this historic State House, under the shadow of the great bell which had tolled from the tower a proclamation of the liberty he had helped to create. The early days of Congress, stormy with dissensions, and later the long-drawn-out arguments which forged a new Federal Constitution were among the doctor's experiences. He had made countless speeches in this building. His career, along with those of his close friends John Adams, Thomas Jefferson, and the respected Dr. Franklin, seemed significantly imbedded in the old red brick structure.

Glories of the past were of small practical value. The question now was whether this case of his would mark another step in American tradition.

The room and galleries were crowded. Most of the spectators were men—lawyers, government people, newspaper representatives, those who were special partisans for one side or the other. But chiefly the onlookers were just the curious.

The doctor felt interested glances in his direction. He

7

did not turn his head but walked steadily through the crowds toward the front of the courtroom. Julia was already there, holding a place for him. Beside her sat their fifteen-year-old daughter Mary, and next to her Richard, his second oldest son, who at nineteen had established himself as a lawyer in his own right. Richard had a professional as well as a family interest in the case.

Rush slipped into his seat and smiled quickly at his wife. She responded with a gentle pressure against his shoulder.

In their years of marriage, the Rushes had faced the fullest measures of life's painfulness as well as happiness. They had gone through the War of Independence, yellow-fever epidemics, the storms of professional criticism, and lately the onslaughts of Peter Porcupine. On occasion the doctor believed he suffered the torments of a modern Job. At the same time he never forgot that he was supported by the steadfastness of a Ruth.

Clad in the black robes of their profession, the lawyers bent over tables as they sorted files of papers taken from green bags. While chancery and common-law practitioners always carried red bags, the color green was the typical badge for lawyers in the higher ranks of the legal profession. As plaintiff, Benjamin Rush had four lawyers. William Cobbett as defendant retained three. Together, the two sets of counsel on this case represented the best talent practicing before the Pennsylvania bar.

Chief counsel for Rush was Joseph Hopkinson, a young lawyer for whom this was the first really important case of his life. The year before, during the crisis of imminent war with France, Hopkinson had gained for himself extralegal fame by writing the patriotic popular song, "Hail Columbia."

Hopkinson looked up from his papers and saw Rush enter the courtroom. He nodded greeting, and left the

8

table where he was working. With quick strides he crossed to the doctor and his family. The lawyer bowed deferentially to Mrs. Rush, smiled at Mary and Richard. Rush stood up, and the two men shook hands.

Richard stood, too, listening eagerly.

"We have the case well prepared, Doctor," Hopkinson said in a low voice. "All of us are hopeful. You heard that Mr. Cobbett has gone to New York?"

Rush raised his eyebrows. "Cobbett gone to New York?"

"Yes, five days ago. We have no valid explanation. Perhaps he thought there would be another postponement of the trial, or perhaps he is too sure of himself. In any case, we hope to give him an unpleasant surprise."

"*I* am surprised he has gone," Rush said. "I hope it is a good omen, not a bad one."

"We will try to make it a good one, Doctor."

Hopkinson bowed again, and went back to the counsels' table, his black robes rustling. A faint musty smell of dye from the robes lingered after him.

Rush sat down again. He glanced at Richard, who was definitely puzzled. "Cobbett gone to New York!" Richard whispered. "Strange!"

The doctor nodded agreement. So the Porcupine had not stayed to fight his own cause. The very fact of it made Rush uneasy. It made him angry, too. The heavy-set, arrogant Englishman had gone off contemptuously, leaving his lawyers to fight his battle as if the case meant nothing to him at all. Leaving the city amounted to Porcupine's supreme gesture of scorn.

The trial had been delayed in coming before the jury for more than two years. Rush brought action first against William Cobbett in October, 1797. That year's yellow-fever epidemic was at its worst then. For weeks preceding through the summer and autumn Cobbett's newspaper, *Porcupine's Gazette,* had let loose upon the doctor a storm of vilification and abuse unparalleled in any records. Under the blast Rush's patients deserted him. His friends turned away. He had been held up to the most savage mockery before the whole city—before the whole nation actually, for the British William Cobbett had made himself more popular and widely read than any other writer in America.

Rush stood almost alone defending his medical practice and system against a torrent of published scorn probably exceeding anything a man ever had to bear. At the same time Philadelphians around him were dying by hundreds. Charging Cobbett with libel was Dr. Rush's final desperate act of self-defense.

Yet the lawyers advised against bringing the lawsuit at all. Ever since the famous John Peter Zenger case of 1734, which established in colonial New York the idea of press freedom, juries had been zealous in defending the right. A number of cases had gone in favor of publishers. Most state constitutions guaranteed freedom of the press, and in 1791 the Bill of Rights pledged freedom of speech and press. It was a flowing tide of publishers' license, and newspapers could print practically what they pleased. For publishers to plead truth as defense was scarcely necessary.

In this atmosphere of liberty to print anything, personal attacks were splashed over newspapers. The custom of firing scurrilous epithets back and forth through journalistic columns became a universal habit. Benjamin Rush was not unique in being a target of newspaper calumny. But most of the published name-calling and character-smearing was done in the name of politics. Rush was not a politician. He was a physician.

William Cobbett, an erstwhile language tutor, had more or less by accident found himself in his special profession. He had jumped into the thick of the American political fight. He was an Englishman, and made himself the political defender in America of his king and country. An enemy of Britain became an enemy of Cobbett. Sentiment in America, especially in Philadelphia, had not recovered from the twenty-year-old bitterness of the War of Independence. Cobbett charged like an angry bull into this hornet's nest of anti-British opinion in the capital city.

Politics at that time gradually had drawn up from utmost confusion into two clearly defined factions. Each faction had a popular personality at its head—Alexander Hamilton, leader of the Federalist party, and Thomas Jefferson of the Democratic-Republicans.

The division between these two parties lay in a deep difference of political philosophy. Hamilton's Federalists believed in strong central government control. They did not rely on the common people as the foundation of government. They wanted to see voting power limited to the educated, intelligent—so they believed—groups of citizens. This system still prevailed in England, where only the higher-ranking classes held rights to vote for their government.

Jefferson's Democratic-Republicans, on the other hand, believed in less central government control, a broader base for opportunity and wealth, greater individual responsibility for the entire population. They placed their faith in all the people to govern themselves. A definition for the philosophy of each political party could state that the Hamiltonians advocated government *for* the people, the Jeffersonians *by* the people.

By the nature of their beliefs, the Federalists were thrown toward affinity with the monarchy government of Britain, and the Democratic-Republicans toward the democracy—"liberty and equality"—for which the French

11

Revolution was aiming. The issues sharply divided Americans, and created a chasm of pro-English and pro-French sympathies.

The issue of "republican" Jeffersonian belief led to the Democratic-Republican party being known as the "French party." Conversely, Hamiliton's Federalists were called the "British party."

The English newspaper writer fell naturally into the ranks of the Federalists. He gave voice through his publications to the policies of Hamilton, the conservative who so adamantly opposed Jeffersonian democracy. The power of Hamilton's forces was tremendous. His philosophy nearly did win out over Jefferson's. The whole destiny of the United States might have been different.

It was strange that Cobbett took Hamilton's conservative position. As a youth in England, he heard his farmer father talk in sympathy with the Americans during the Revolution. He himself once planned to become a citizen of the United States. And at the time of the Rush trial Cobbett himself never would have believed that one day in England he would be jailed for attacking the government of the very same English king he now so vigorously supported.

The whole story was strange, even to the fact that William Cobbett, under his pen name of Peter Porcupine, waged such a campaign against the Philadelphia physician who was not a politician at all.

But Dr. Rush had never been a man who could live long without controversy.


## 2   *A Headstrong Man*

BENJAMIN RUSH inherited two conflicting aspects of personality. He was born in 1746 into a conservative farming and trade family at Byberry, twelve miles up the Delaware from Philadelphia. He was the oldest of the fifth generation of Rushes in America, counting back to 1683, the same year in which William Penn founded Philadelphia. His father, by reputation a man of scrupulous honesty and industrious character, died when young Ben was six. His mother brought him up in the strict Presbyterian manner, sending him at age eight to West Nottingham Academy at Rising Sun, Maryland, and then to the College of New Jersey at Princeton. He graduated with his B.A. at the age of fifteen, firm in acceptance of the usual and established order of tradition.

Yet even out of his family background Rush inherited the sense of rebellion that helped him to become such a contentious figure. On the wall of the family farmhouse hung a sword that had belonged to the boy's great-grandfather, the original Rush to come to America. Captain John Rush had been a cavalry officer in Oliver Cromwell's army of revolt. Young Ben dreamed of pride and glory when he looked at that sword.

When Rush began his Philadelphia career by becoming an apprentice to Dr. John Redman, senior physician of the city, there were no medical schools in America. The first was not established until 1765, as part of the College of Philadelphia. The practice of physic, as it was called, had developed slowly in the colonies. In the early years, medical care was administered by the clergy or by housewives who had picked up the simplest remedies through experience and intuition.

Only by going abroad after an initial apprenticeship could a hopeful young man expect to study for a career in physic. The center of professional learning was then at the University of Edinburgh. After five apprentice years under Dr. Redman, Rush spent four more of study in Scotland, until he earned his M.D. degree.

In Edinburgh, Rush learned more than medicine. He had his initiation into political philosophy. Years before the Revolution, he discovered that the arbitrary right of kings to govern the people of a nation could be questioned. An Englishman, a fellow student at the medical college, opened his eyes. The young man's name was Bostock, and he cried to Rush, "I had an ancestor with Cromwell even as you did. They fought for the same kind of *republican* principles in which I believe myself. To this day I challenge the authority of kings. Government must be *by the people!*"

Rush had never heard the rights of monarchy so outspokenly challenged. The policies of Parliament were disputed in America, yes, but not the power of the King himself. His eyes widened. "What are you saying?" he asked. "You can't question the government of our King—"

"Kings be damned! Because they *inherit* power, do they *deserve* it? Absurd!"

"But the King *is* government," Rush protested. "He is as essential to political order as the sun is essential to the solar system."

"Is any form of government rational that is not based on the will of the people?" Bostock waved his arms. "Government must be derived from the suffrage of people who are subject to it. Do you blindly accept the rule of a king just because he was born a king? You fool!"

"In America we resisted the Stamp Act," Rush said. "It was not because of the King, but on account of the ministers who passed it—"

"Pfaa!" Bostock shouted. He added, slowly, for emphasis, "Recognize, my friend, that established order *must* be doubted, whether of kings or anything else. Tear yourself loose, my friend, and try to find the truth."

"But then," Rush replied thoughtfully, "I should

14

suspect error in everything I have been taught, and in everything I've believed."

"Nothing can be true to *you*," Bostock said, "if you accept only the word of other men."

"Does that make me a skeptic?"

Bostock grinned. "Hardly. But make up your own mind."

From that moment Rush never accepted other men's beliefs without careful personal conviction of his own. He sought out truth for himself, energetically, whether in medicine or politics or anything else. This guiding force made him question all medical theory up to his time.

Of Bostock, little else is known except that he became a physician in England and died early in life. His fame rests on the fire he kindled in his student friend.

Another Englishman helped Rush along the road to political rebellion. From Edinburgh, as a young graduate doctor, he visited London. There he was introduced to the man who was rousing the masses of England against the King's power—the famous John Wilkes, Radical and a member of Parliament. Rush met Wilkes in jail—a very luxurious kind of confinement, the Philadelphian found to his astonishment. Wilkes was imprisoned for, in effect, calling George III a liar.

Because he was a ranking political prisoner, Wilkes had special jail privileges. These included a private apartment, the right to entertain guests, and the means of giving lavish dinner parties. These things impressed Rush, but even more he was struck by the hideous physical appearance of the rabble-rousing Wilkes—nose flat to deformity, jaw twisted, complexion sallow. Yet, contrary to stories, the doctor found him well mannered, fashionably dressed, gracious to his visitor from overseas. Benjamin Rush looked with fascination at the man who

15

personified a new force let loose in the world. It was a force demanding rights in government for every citizen, calling for revolution even by violence if necessary.

Wilkes expressed his friendship to America. He had a letter from the Sons of Liberty in Boston. Rush did not know the signers, among whom was a John Adams. The doctor came away from that meeting fired by one particular sentence of Wilkes: *If you can but preserve an equality among one another, you will always be free in spite of everything.*

The young doctor returned to Philadelphia in 1769 to become a firebrand of patriotism. He was one of the small nucleus of patriots early demanding separation from Britain. His patience ran short with those who advocated caution. In thoroughly unmedical manner he made speeches, wrote newspaper articles calling for complete independence. Before the Boston affair ever happened, Philadelphians had their own "Tea Party." On Christmas Day, 1773, the ship *Polly* arrived in port with a cargo of tea to be taxed under the new English law. Without unloading a pound, it was forced to sail away by a group of the "Sons of Liberty." Benjamin Rush was there.

He saw the need for a pamphlet to urge Americans toward independence. The doctor was prudent enough at this point to protect his professional standing by not writing such a piece himself, even anonymously. By chance one day, in a bookstore, he met a newcomer to Philadelphia, an Englishman who came to America with a letter of introduction from Benjamin Franklin in London. The stranger hoped to earn a living by tutoring young ladies and gentlemen in geography. His name was Thomas Paine.

The meeting might have ended uneventfully except that Paine was writing a newspaper essay against slavery of Negroes. Rush had written similar ones. Paine, it developed, also shared the doctor's ideas on American

16

independence from Britain. Rush jumped at this opportunity. Write a pamphlet, he urged Paine, on the subject of separation. Paine agreed. Rush helped with ideas, criticism, even supplied the title of the pamphlet: *Common Sense*. The doctor was the one to find a publisher willing to print such a treasonable manuscript. Paine's *Common Sense* was, as Benjamin Franklin described it, "a pamphlet that had prodigious effects." Washington wrote of it, "I find *Common Sense* is working a powerful change in the minds of men." John Adams said, "Dr. Rush put him [Paine] upon writing on the subject, furnished him with the arguments which have been urged in Congress a hundred times, and gave him his title of *Common Sense.*"

Rush went on to be appointed to Congress in July, 1776, shortly after independence was proclaimed. He was in time to sign the Declaration as a representative of Pennsylvania. He inscribed his name, then handed the pen over to Benjamin Franklin whose signature appears just under that of Benjamin Rush.

Rush served in Washington's army for a time as physician-general in charge of hospital patients. He found the entire medical department of the army corrupted with graft and incompetence. He blamed his commanding officer, the director-general of the department, Dr. William Shippen. Shippen was also of Philadelphia and Rush's senior by ten years. The quarrel between the two physicians arising from Rush's criticism grew into a lifelong rupture which had echoes even in the lawsuit against Cobbett twenty years later. Rush was dropped from the Revolutionary Army, although he never ceased to blame Shippen for the deaths, through neglect and fraud, of thousands of hospitalized soldiers.

"I find from examining Dr. Shippen's return of the numbers who die in hospitals," he wrote to an army

17

general, "that I was mistaken in the account I gave of that matter in my letters to you. From his return of December last I find very few have died in proportion to the number I have mentioned. All I can say in apology for this mistake is that I was deceived by counting the number of coffins that were daily put underground. From their weight and smell I am persuaded they contained hospital patients in them, and if they were not dead I hope some steps will be taken for the future to prevent and punish the crime of burying the Continental soldiers alive."

Rush's headstrong personality led him into controversy through most of his life. His Revolutionary activities alienated him from conservative Philadelphians. His liberal political views and intense efforts for the adoption of both the Federal and Pennsylvania State constitutions angered men of highest influence. His social-reform ambitions against slavery, capital punishment, and liquor made him unpopular with special groups. The advances he sponsored in American education, including the founding of Dickinson College at Carlisle, Pennsylvania, ran into opposition from political and religious factions. He antagonized the medical profession. He estranged himself from his patients.

The doctor never rested easily when his principles were in danger.

3    *"Oyez! Oyez! Oyez!"*

A RUSTLE of expectancy swept through the courtroom. The jurymen were moving into their seats.

The twelve men had been selected from a special panel. Some Rush knew to be Federalists, others Democratic-Republicans. The lawyers had warned the doctor that politics might easily creep into this trial, even so far as to bring about a party-affiliation decision.

Rush's nerves were on edge. What had been the worth of his life, he thought, that judgment of him should come to rest in the hands of these twelve men? A majority of Philadelphians had already condemned him. Was it possible that a jury of citizens would decide in his favor? The controversy between Cobbett and himself included so many aspects. It had come to represent a common conflict in which most of the people of the city, even the jurors themselves, had a share.

"Oyez! Oyez! Oyez! . . ." The court bailiff's chant carried over the buzzing conversation filling the room. "In this Supreme Court of the State of Pennsylvania . . ."

Feet shuffled, chairs moved. The throng of spectators, the jury, rose from their seats. The lawyers came to attention. A door opened and the three justices of the Court solemnly entered. Each wore the judiciary robes of red, with white wigs on their heads. As was customary, the senior justice, Edward Shippen, wore his hat. Shippen was a dignified man over seventy, due in a few days to be appointed Chief Justice by Governor McKean, himself the Chief Justice until the recent Pennsylvania election for the governorship. Associate justices were Jasper Yates and Thomas Smith.

They took their places on the bench. The room subsided, the gavel pounded. Court was in session.

"Dr. Benjamin Rush versus William Cobbett, action on the case for a libel," the clerk called out.

Hopkinson, chief counsel, began the case for the doctor. He moved out from his table to the space before the bench and jury box. With a preliminary bow to the judges, he faced the twelve men.

"Gentlemen of the jury," he began slowly, "it is my duty to open this case to you on the part of the plaintiff, Dr. Rush. In discharging this duty I shall beg leave to extend it somewhat beyond its usual limits in ordinary cases. I shall not be content with merely reading the declaration to you and stating its point, but shall also take the liberty of opening to you the views and dispositions with which this action has been brought, and some of the leading principles on which it will be supported."

Hopkinson paused. He put his hands behind his back, among the folds of the robe.

"The action now before you is an action of slander brought by Dr. Benjamin Rush, who has long been a distinguished ornament of our city, against William Cobbett, the printer and publisher of a newspaper under the name of *Porcupine's Gazette.*" No slight cause could bring a man of Dr. Rush's character into this or any other kind of competition with a man of William Cobbett's character, the lawyer said. It was not to indulge a fondness for controversy or to gratify a revengeful disposition that the doctor sought justice and protection for his reputation. "Dr. Rush is as well known for his peaceful habits and his amiable manner as William Cobbett is for malignant disposition and inveterate hate. He comes here impressed with high duties. To the *laws of his country* he owes a duty that they shall not be violated. To his *fellow citizens* he owes a duty to bring punishment—" Hopkinson's voice rose urgently and he pounded one hand with his fist— "and if possible suppress an abandoned and dangerous offender who tramples over truth, decency, and character with a tiger's stride, who assaults with venomous fury the most sacred bands of social order and peace!"

The lawyer walked back to his table and picked up a paper. He would read the declaration of the case, he said. He quoted from a formal statement listing the charges which had brought the suit to trial. A selection of passages from *Porcupine's Gazette* was declared libelous.

"Mr. Cobbett has called Dr. Rush a 'quack,' a 'medical

puffer,' and 'empyric,' " Hopkinson told the jury. He read: " '*The times are ominous, indeed, when quack to quack cries purge and bleed.*' "

He paused. Then he said slowly, "The defendent has in effect accused Dr. Rush of *murder,* and not only the doctor but those who have profited by his teaching." He read a quotation:

" '*Dr. Rush in that emphatical style which is peculiar to himself calls mercury the Samson of medicine. In his hands and those of his partisans it may indeed be justly compared to Samson: for I verily believe they have slain more Americans with it than ever Samson slew of the Philistines. The Israelite slew his thousands, but the Rushites have slain their tens of thousands.*' "

Another article quoted by Hopkinson referred to newspapers all over the country which Cobbett claimed were spreading news of how Rush's methods were used everywhere by other doctors. Cobbett pointed out, " '—*the arts that our remorseless Bleeder is making use of to puff off his preposterous practice. He has his partisans in almost every quarter of the country. There is scarcely a page of any newspaper that I can see which has the good fortune to escape the poison of their prescriptions. Blood, blood! Still they cry more blood! In every sentence they menace our poor veins. Their language is as frightful to the ears of the alarmed multitudes as is the raven's croak to those of the sickly flock.*' "

Rush's face reddened. He watched stonily as Hopkinson walked up and down, reading more. Yet even the official document listed a mere fraction of the violent, abusive, and biting expressions by which Cobbett had held up the doctor's reputation to sarcastic laughter.

Hopkinson warned the jurors that political feelings might enter the trial. "Political parties in our country

21

have become wrought up to such fury that every action of a man's life from the most important to the most obscure and trifling is traced to party motives and party principles. His friends and enemies, his connections in business, almost the color of the cloth he wears and the diet he feeds on, are ascribed to his party and political principles." He paused again, then added a caustic understatement, "This is an unhappy state of things!"

He himself was not to be influenced in the case by politics. But he said to the jurors, concerning the defendant, "Doubtless his dark and virulent spirit prepares some attack which his insufferable arrogance informs him will be formidable and destructive to lawyers, court, and jury that shall dare to do him justice. For myself I declare, if the declaration be necessary, that there is not in the bounds of creation that thing so feeble or so vile that I should hold it in greater contempt than the resentment of William Cobbett.

"I will answer that you *will* not be driven from your duties or your oaths by a fear of being placed on *his* black list. He has the unquenchable and vindictive spirit of an inquisitor, but wanting all power it is harmless and contemptible. The ridiculous vanity of this man and his ignorance of his true situation in this country have led him into an opinion that his voice is the voice of Fate! This is an error which it lies with the public to correct."

Hopkinson went on to another subject, the main legal issue of the trial:

"Gentlemen, no subject of legal inquiry has excited more anxiety among the people of every free country, or received more frequent discussion in every possible form of argument, than the *liberty of the press*. Yet perhaps no subject is now more remote from a general understanding or settled opinion." It was difficult to draw a line between safe use and insufferable abuse of this liberty, he said.
22

"But, gentlemen, this mighty uproar about the liberty of the press, and all the violence, declamation, and invective that it has excited, touch not the case of *private slander.*"

Hopkinson viewed the true liberty of the press as a lofty citadel from which the people surveyed the conduct of those who governed them. From it they could crush ambitious oppression or unprincipled designs. Before the liberty of the press the wicked stood appalled, but the good flourished. Yet the safety of this citadel and of this country was more in danger from treachery of pretended friends than the violence of open foes.

"That which was intended for the public good is the prostituted instrument of private malice. That which was erected for the salvation of a people becomes the foul avenger of a villain's wrath. That thunder which stood ready to assert violated rights and protect the liberties of millions is pointed with deadly vengeance against the domestic happiness of some virtuous family, the private peace of some deserving citizen. Is *this* the liberty of the press?

"The high-toned and pretended sons of liberty, who bawl incessantly about the rights of the press while they blacken it with their detestable crimes, who tell you it is sacred while they are plunging it in disgrace, who under its name and sanction practice the most abandoned licentiousness and invade our most important and valuable rights, must be laid low, or they will work a fatal ruin to the liberty they abuse."

Benjamin Rush looked around the courtroom. Justice Smith stared immovably up at the ceiling. Shippen leaned forward on his elbows, watching Hopkinson attentively, noting every word. Yates sat back with his eyes closed. The jury listened as if spellbound by the lawyer's rise and fall of voice. Julia was motionless with a face turned pale.

23

Joseph Hopkinson leaned over the jury box and seemed to speak directly to each man in turn.

"The attack made on Dr. Rush is of the most deadly and violent kind that malice could invent, or abandoned depravity execute. He is accused of murder, of destroying the lives of his fellow citizens in a time of dreadful calamity. It is then fair and necessary to inquire—first, what was the conduct of Dr. Rush during that calamity? Has it merited reproach or applause? If the former, the offense of William Cobbett is extenuated though not justified. If the latter, it is aggravated beyond all example. Second, what inducement or motive had William Cobbett for this attack? If a desire to inform the public mind on an interesting subject, his offense is extenuated—but not justified. If private and political malice, it is aggravated."

Having so summarized his case, Hopkinson walked for a moment across the floor. He returned to the jury box with shoulders hunched as if about to spring. He recalled the undaunted conduct of the immortal Hippocrates in Athens during times of pestilence. "He endured the extremes of fatigue and distress to assist and deliver his perishing fellow citizens. How like this was the conduct of Dr. Rush in the memorable and dreadful year 1793! He stood then foremost and almost alone to encounter and arrest the ravages of death. Hundreds of our fellow citizens sought relief as well from the Christian charity of his heart as from the powerful application of his skill.

"Gentlemen, let us not forget the days of difficulty and distress. This flourishing city, where health, business, and pleasure gave joy to every heart, became at once silent as a wilderness, the solemn habitation of disease and death. No longer the noise of business was heard through our streets, or the sprightly notes of mirth, but the dull sounds of heavy hearse. The lamentations of the wretched

24

struck an uneasy terror to the soul. The day and night were the same. The rising sun brought no comfort, no joy to the afflicted, nor night its usual rest. All was sadness, ruin, and despair. Commerce bent her sails for happier ports. Your warehouses no longer received or distributed the wealth of nations. The temples of God were closed, and it was dangerous to meet together even to implore from Divine Mercy an end to our sufferings.

*"Where then was Dr. Rush? Where was this man and how was he employed,* who has been treated as a very cutthroat, a worthless and abandoned vagabond who disgraces the community which tolerates his existence? Need I tell you where he was? God forbid that you should have forgotten—"

He stopped and waited, as if allowing time for the memories to flood back into the jurymen's minds. Then he said in a voice so low that the spectators had to strain to hear:

"Let me call upon you, gentlemen, by the just heavens to consider this as no common case. Let me call upon you to feel yourselves entrusted with one of the most important decisions that has ever yet been submitted to any court in any country.

"By your decision we stand or fall!"

No one in that courtroom, if he had been a Philadelphian in 1793, could have forgotten the summer of that year. The jurors, the judges, most of the spectators had lived through it. Every scene of horror, every shriek of pain must have been etched so starkly on men's minds that they could never escape the memories.

They could not have forgotten Dr. Benjamin Rush's part in the yellow-fever epidemic, or the bitter dispute among the city's physicians which had not been settled up to this very day of the lawsuit. . . .

# The Fever

# 4

## Miasma from the River Front

ON Monday, August 19, 1793, Philadelphia lay in the grip of a heat wave. Dr. Rush had been summoned to an emergency consultation in the case of a woman sick with fever. Fevers were common enough at that time of year, and Dr. Rush had no reason to think this call was out of the ordinary routine.

Already in attendance were Dr. Hugh Hodge and Dr. John Foulke, the latter a one-time student of Rush. He met the two men at the patient's house on Water Street, north of Arch and close to the river. The sick woman was one Catherine LeMaigre, wife of a Philadelphia merchant.

The moment he entered the patient's room, Dr. Rush's habitual frown deepened. The close air was heavy with an unusual and unnatural smell of sickness. Something stirred in his memory, but he could not place at the moment what it was.

The patient rolled on the bed with agony. She had thrown off the covers and clutched at her stomach while sweat poured from her flushed face.

"Dr. Rush," she groaned hoarsely, "it's the burning down here—" Even as she spoke she retched and vomited bile into a basin on the bed.

"She's been doing this regular," the woman with her said. "She's in bad pain, sir."

The woman quickly took the basin from the room as Rush sat by the bedside. The other doctors stood back. Dr. Rush patted the patient's arm reassuringly, at the same time noting the inflamed eyes and their yellowish cast. In his usually careful manner, he took both wrists at once, one in each hand, to feel the pulse. It was rapid, tense. After each fourth or fifth beat the heart gave an intermittent jump.

"Please, may I see your tongue?" he asked gently. In this case, unlike ordinary fevers, a suspicion of a dry black streak ran down the middle.

He sat back in his chair. The sight of approaching death was familiar enough to Benjamin Rush. For thirty-one years he had been in the medical profession. He had seen epidemics and disasters, slept side by side with wounded soldiers after battles of the Revolution, witnessed untold horrors during the war. Yet this case of Catherine LeMaigre struck him with an unexpectedly cold chill.

That strange sickroom smell. Suddenly he remembered all the way back to his first year as a young student apprentice in Philadelphia.

The woman returned with the basin. Dr. Rush rose to his feet and glanced at the other physicians.

"You are giving cordials and tonics?" he asked them. "My only suggestion is to increase the strength of the doses."

30

Dr. Hodge nodded. The patient lay with eyes closed, breathing heavily. Even as the attending woman replaced the basin on the bed, Mrs. LeMaigre vomited again.

The doctors left the room, walked downstairs in silence. By a jerk of his head, Rush indicated the parlor. He entered, and the others followed. They closed the door.

Rush's thoughts were running with lightning speed. Several facts lined up side by side in his mind, but for the moment they did not seem to fit together. He glanced from one doctor to the other.

"Unhappily, I do not believe much can be done for the patient," he said. He kept his voice low, speaking formally. Even in ordinary circumstances he was a formal man. This was a house of sickness. "Obviously," he went on, "the tonics and cordials are of no purpose."

They agreed. Both physicians knew Rush well. All three were members of Philadelphia's College of Physicians.

Hodge had respected Rush enough to call him in as a physician to his own family. Exactly two weeks before, his small daughter had come down with a fever of the bilious kind. Rush attended her, but after two days of illness the child died. Her skin had turned yellow. If Dr. Hodge felt any blame toward Rush, he had not indicated it.

Dr. Rush crossed to the window looking out on Water Street. A wagon rumbled by on its way to the river wharves only a few doors distant. Then he turned quickly to Hodge. Usually he wasted few words, and little time. His manner was precise as his thoughts, quick and intense.

"I've seen an unusual number of these bilious fevers lately," he said. "The symptoms show uncommon malignity." He went on seriously, "I must tell you both I suspect all is not right in our city."

Hodge's face moved slightly. He could have been

31

remembering his little girl. Rush himself thought of his own children.

"As a matter of fact," Hodge replied steadily, "a fever of the most malignant kind has carried off four or five persons within sight of this house on Water Street. One died within twelve hours of the first attack."

"The neighborhood has been cursed lately," Dr. Foulke added. "Beside the illness, there has been the smell of that coffee putrefying on Ball's Wharf—"

"Coffee? Putrefying?"

"It was damaged aboard ship coming from the West Indies, and thrown on two of the docks. It has been there since July 24. The whole neighborhood here by the river has been complaining."

"And Ball's Wharf is on a direct line with the Le-Maigre house!" Rush cried. "Of course—there's the fever's origin. The exhalation is in the air!" He raised a finger. "Young M'Nair who died a week ago had been working on that same dock, I remember now. Other cases I've had, I believe I can trace them all to the same source."

The two doctors stared at him, not understanding.

"Gentlemen," Rush said in a voice that trembled slightly, "I have no hesitation now in calling this the bilious remitting *yellow fever*."

Foulke glanced uneasily at Hodge. "I had not thought to connect the two—"

"And if it be so," Rush continued rapidly, "it is highly contagious, as well as mortal. It could spread through the city far beyond Water Street."

Dr. Hodge cleared his throat. "It is not for us to cause undue alarm," he said cautiously. "More likely these are cases of unusually severe bilious fevers in the ordinary sense of the summer."

Rush was impatiently sure of his ground. "I hope you may be right," he said. "But I remember the yellow

32

fever of 1762. The same sickroom smell. Twenty people a day died of it then. Now the city is much larger. I have the worst apprehension, gentlemen. May the hand of the Lord be with us in days to come."

He left Hodge and Foulke standing aghast. Taking his high-crowned hat from the front hall, he went out into the heat of the street. For a moment Rush paused. He looked in the direction of Ball's Wharf.

The putrefying coffee—of course. A miasma fouled the air. It supplied the reason, and the disjointed pieces fitted together.

The doctor untied his horse from the hitching post and climbed into his light chaise. He drove rapidly down Second Street toward Market, past the house where Benjamin Franklin once lived, and by towering Christ Church with its trees and yard.

He noticed people stepping over rotting refuse in the gutters—discarded vegetable scraps, decaying fish, dog excrement, a dead cat. The doctor shuddered. Such filth bred contagion. If ever the miasma from the decaying coffee seeped out through the city, the results could be catastrophic.

The summer had been dry to the point of drought. No rain washed away the dirt of the streets. The Delaware River, shrunk back in its channel leaving muddy banks exposed, increased the potential danger as did dried-up ponds around the city.

Dr. Rush felt the impending crisis, and already guessed his helplessness before it. He could never avoid the sense of responsibility to mankind.

Suddenly he saw an acquaintance crossing Second Street. He pulled in the horse.

"Good day, Doctor," the friend greeted him. "Dry weather continues, doesn't it?"

Rush did not smile. "Unfortunately, yes." He leaned

33

forward in the carriage. "Sir, I've discovered yellow fever in town. If the weather doesn't change, it may spread through the city."

His friend stepped back. "Yellow fever!"

"Most malignant and contagious," the doctor warned. "I urge you to get yourself and your family quickly out of town."

"But—"

"So far it's confined to Water Street. There is no guessing what may happen."

The man was pale. "Yes, Doctor. I don't know how I can go—my business, you see, but—yes, I'll tell my wife at once."

Dr. Rush nodded. "I'd advise the same for everyone," he said.

"Thank you, Doctor." The man stared after Rush as the carriage went on. He turned to someone else passing along the street. "Did you hear what the doctor said?"

To several others Rush gave the same news and advice. The only sure way to avoid the contagion was to leave the city, he told them. Then he drove on toward his own house on Walnut Street.

Already his warning of contagion must be racing through the streets. No more effective way could be found to let Philadelphians know what they faced. His name would attach importance to the report. It was well. The more persons who left town, the less the danger of the disease spreading.

5    "I Believe We Are Near to
    a Disaster Here"

AT HOME he met his sister in the front hall. The doctor had already sent his wife and four of the children to his mother-in-law's house at Princeton for the summer. He was especially glad now that they were safely out in the country. Only the two older boys, John and Richard, and the youngest son Ben, were still with him.

Rebecca Wallace, his sister, was keeping house for the doctor and for his mother also staying with them. Rush was particularly fond of his sister. A widow, she had been married twice, and her calm, somewhat reserved nature came as much from sorrow in her life as from her own personality. For her to keep house seemed like days of old, for she had done the same thing when Rush came back from Edinburgh to start practice.

Her first glance at his face told her of trouble. His eyes were averted, and tight, nervous veins stood out on the back of his hands.

"Something is wrong? Your patient—"

The doctor looked at her squarely. "I would like you to take Mother from the city soon. Go out to the country."

"Why?"

He drew a breath. "I believe we are near to a disaster here. The yellow fever is in town."

She waited a moment before answering. "Will it be that bad?"

"I fear so. Perhaps not, but—"

"What of little Ben and the older boys?"

"I will send them away, too."

Rebecca smiled. "Do you think for one moment Mother would go? Or I?"

Dr. Rush frowned. "That is not the point. I would not want you to risk—"

"What of you?"

He stared at her as if he could not quite understand. Then he smiled a little. "I profess to believe in and try to imitate a Saviour," he said, "who did not *risk* but who *gave* His life, not for His friends but His enemies."

35

Rebecca smiled, too. "And I will not leave. My life is of no consequence to me, or to the public. I will stay here and take care of my brother. His life may be useful to many."

Dr. Rush chuckled, then said, "There is no more use in suggesting that Mother should go than you. Shall we say nothing of this to her for a day or so?"

"I agree," Rebecca said. "Perhaps it will not be so bad."

"Would to God," Rush said.

He left his hat in the hall. The doctor used his house as office and shop as well as living quarters for his family. Usually he received patients in his parlor, assisted by apprentices—young men from eighteen to twenty years of age—who came in each day to work and study. Eleven-year-old Peter did minor chores, and the only other household servant was Marcus, a Negro man.

Rush went back to the kitchen. He found his mother helping Marcus with a pastry. The servant had been suffering with influenza and still felt shaky on his feet.

"I'm glad you're home, my son," the elder Mrs. Rush said. She wore a white hat on her head, and a long apron to protect her brown silk gown. "I saw Peter leading off your horse. You've had a long day in the heat."

The kitchen seemed hotter than outdoors. Dr. Rush wiped his brow, but his mother did not seem disturbed in the least by the weather. She was like that.

"May I have a dish of tea?" he asked.

"Of course. I've made it already. Sit down, Benjamin, right here at the table."

She crossed the room for the teapot. At seventy-six, Mrs. John Rush was as active and perceptive as ever she had been when solely responsible for bringing up and educating six small children. Rush believed that he owed
36

all his faith in God and integrity of purpose, the balances to his impetuous nature, to his mother's firm example. She came back to the table, looking sharply at her son. "You're concerned with something."

"Concerned? Not in the least. Thank you for the tea."

"What is it, Benjamin?"

"You remember Mrs. LeMaigre? I believe she is dying."

"What a pity. She's young. I am so sorry."

As he poured the tea, Benjamin Rush knew she was standing behind him, thinking. She understood more than she ever said. He had not really kept anything from her, not anything at all.

"When you write to your dear Julia," she said after a moment, "tell her we are well. Tell her Rebecca and I are taking care of you and the boys."

"Yes, Dr. Rush," Marcus added eagerly from near the stove. "You can tell Mis' Rush I be better now."

"I will, Marcus." Rush looked up gratefully at his mother. His usually taut face relaxed. "I'll tell Mrs. Rush."

He wrote to Julia almost every night before going to bed. Then usually he added a postscript the following morning before starting the day's work.

That night at the writing table in their bedroom on the second floor, Benjamin Rush was thinking. He had not started his letter yet. If the fever became prevalent, he would be unable to leave the city for the several weeks he had planned to be with his family at Princeton.

The window was open in the bedroom. A night breeze stirred the candle flame. Outside, the stars shone brightly. It was late as usual, for Benjamin Rush liked to

37

keep up with his studies in the evening hours. He heard the watchman pass by at midnight. The rest of the city seemed asleep.

God preserve Philadelphia from the poison that begins to stir within it, he thought.

He was tired, but he did not feel like sleeping. His mind under tension was too active. He was concerned about the safety of the three boys still with him in Philadelphia. The older ones he would send to their mother, but he would not risk Ben's taking the long trip. The little boy could stay with someone on a country farm nearer at hand.

Mosquitoes were coming through the open window, attracted by the candlelight. Rush blew out the flame to sit a while in the dark. Nostalgically he longed for Julia's presence with him tonight, the touch of her hand. He was not given to romantic sentiment, but his happiest times were with Julia. . . .

They had been married in January, 1776, the year of American independence. He claimed he was first attracted to her because she liked a sermon. Actually, Julia had reminded him of someone else, a girl of Scotland whom he met while in Edinburgh.

The Scottish girl, Lady Jane Leslie, daughter of the Earl of Leven, was fifteen when he was a medical student of twenty-two. He heard her sing an old ballad in Edinburgh's Nicholson Square—"The Birks of Endermay." The interlude with Lady Jane was laced with love and music and a romantic game between the pair based on a currently popular song from the play, then new, by Oliver Goldsmith, *The Vicar of Wakefield*. The song concerned two parted lovers named Edwin and Angelina. Perhaps the Lady Jane knew from the beginning that their destinies were not together, but in any case they played the

38

parts of the forlorn Angelina and Edwin even in correspondence long after.

Seven years later, on a summer evening, he met Julia. This was 1775. Dr. Rush paid a visit to Princeton, staying with Mr. and Mrs. Richard Stockton, friends of college days. They met his stagecoach at a tavern outside Princeton. Richard Stockton was a lawyer and judge, his wife Annice wrote poetry as a hobby. They took him back to their house, the mansion named Morven, set among the pines of Princeton. At the door was a pretty girl of sixteen. "Dr. Rush, our daughter Julia. Perhaps you may remember her—"

He did. They had met once before, under quite different circumstances. With twinkling eyes he reminded her that years earlier he had rescued a four-year-old child from the crush of a crowd emerging from evening commencement at Nassau Hall. He carried her in his arms back to her own home. The child was Julia.

She blushed and laughed, and looked again at the man who had become a serious-minded doctor. Julia was tall, brown-haired, dark-eyed, grave, and demure in the presence of the stranger. He noticed her manners and the correct way she spoke.

In the family gathering that evening, Julia, the eldest daughter, was requested to sing for the guest's entertainment. She would sing a ballad of Scotland, she said. Then Benjamin Rush gasped. *The smiling morn, the breathless spring . . .* " The song was "The Birks of Endermay," the song his Lady Jane had sung in Edinburgh! As he listened he was carried back to the hills of Scotland. This could not be Lady Jane herself, his Angelina? He realized all at once that the girl of Princeton was the same size, the same age as Lady Jane had been then. Even a charming lisp in her voice was the same. The similarity seemed remarkable—but no, the story of Edwin and Angelina was over. This was Princeton. The dark-eyed girl singing was Julia Stockton.

Her song ended. Its melody stayed with him. He made certain to talk with Julia the next day. She spoke of a sermon she had heard, or rather of the preacher who had delivered it. The Reverend Dr. John Witherspoon was then president of the College of New Jersey. Rush had been instrumental in bringing the well-known Presbyterian minister from Paisley, Scotland, to fill the college presidency at Princeton. "He is the best preacher I have ever heard," Julia said sincerely. Perhaps Rush remembered Lady Jane in Scotland saying the same thing about Dr. Witherspoon. Here was another reminder.

That Julia would make such a comment at her age impressed Benjamin Rush as much as anything else. She must have unusual soundness of judgment and correctness of taste, he thought. At that moment he made up his mind.

The following January, in the turmoil of approaching revolution, they were married in Princeton.

Julia Rush found more than the usual handicaps of being a doctor's wife. Not only at sixteen did she begin marriage at the start of a long war, but the temperament of her husband would have taxed the understanding nature of nearly any other woman. He was too energetic, strong-willed, ready to fly into furious battle at the least sign of injustice to anyone. Overly frank, Dr. Rush could win faithful loyalty from a few friends, but more often aggravate hatred of many enemies.

He was an exacting man with specific standards for a wife's perfection. A good wife should have no will of her own, he insisted. Right or wrong, she must be subordinate to her husband, trusting that time would show him his mistakes. Love was less important than esteem and respect. Indeed, he believed, a woman owed nothing to a man for

40

*loving* her. If she had personal charm, he could not withhold his *love*. Love was a selfish passion, and men yielded to it for the sake of receiving not imparting pleasure. A man might insult the woman he loved when he was angry, but never the woman whom he respected and esteemed.

Julia far more than met his specifications. The doctor even wrote to Lady Jane about his wife—he had told Julia the story of Edwin and Angelina. He described Julia, "the friend, the companion, and the wife in the full meaning of each of these words."

In the dark of the Philadelphia night he looked up at the stars over the city. The breeze stirred the strands of hair around his head. "Good night, thou dear right side of my heart," he whispered.

He lit the candle again. He went back to the writing table and took up his pen to begin his letter: "My dear Julia, to prevent your being deceived by reports respecting the sickliness of our city, I sit down at a late hour, and much fatigued, to inform you that a malignant fever has broken out in Water Street between Arch and Race streets . . ."

## 6  *"Dead — Both Dead!"*

PHILADELPHIA waited tensely through the first week of the reported fever. For three or four days nothing much seemed to happen, and the townspeople began to lose their panic. Most of the city's doctors were expressing skepticism. True, there were cases of ordinary fever, but they scorned the idea of a threatened epidemic of yellow fever. Dr. Rush expressed undue alarm, they said.

Meanwhile, the doctor himself was busy with more

cases which he diagnosed as yellow fever, and also with a violent wave of influenza that appeared.

During that week one affair occurred which Rush took time to attend. At a noonday dinner the Negroes of Philadelphia celebrated the roof raising of the First African Church. The doctor had been responsible for the idea of the church, and he had arranged for the construction financing.

Since youthful days Rush had sympathized with Negroes' welfare, and had taken an active part in the slavery controversy. With Benjamin Franklin, he worked for the Abolitionist cause, successfully enough to help abolish slavery in Pennsylvania in 1788. Since then Philadelphia's three thousand freed Negroes had lived in a state of depression. Rush believed a church and adjoining school of their own would go a long way toward improving their condition.

A hundred white persons attended the dinner, too, including many of the carpenters working on the church building. The Negroes waited on them at a long table set under the trees. The dinner was good, the wine of the first quality. For dessert there were melons. From the head of the table, Dr. Rush offered two toasts: "Peace on earth and good will to men," and "May African churches everywhere soon succeed to African bondage."

Afterward the white guests and the Negroes exchanged places at the table. Some of the white people waited on the Negroes. Rush himself and several others sat at the table with the members of the new parish of the African Church. One Billy Gray cried tears of emotion as the event concluded. Absalom Jones, to be the church's minister, was there, and a Negro named Richard Allen.

The windows of the city prison overlooked the scene of the roof raising. Conscious of the inmates' curiosity, Dr. Rush that afternoon sent them a large wheelbarrow full of
42

melons. With the gift went a note requesting the prisoners to remember as they ate the fruit that God still cared for them, and that by this and other acts of kindness performed by His people, God meant to lead them to repentance and happiness.

Dr. Rush had sent similar gifts to prisoners in the past. He referred to them as "my other class of friends, the criminals in the jail."

But on Sunday morning, August 25, Dr. Rush awakened shortly after daybreak to hear Marcus knocking at his bedroom door. Word had come by messenger that the doctor should hurry to two patients on Water Street. A father and son. He had treated both on the day before.

Rush was used to early calls. He kept his clothes ready so he could dress quickly. He was soon downstairs, moving softly so he would not awaken his mother and sister, or the boys. He paused only long enough for a cup of coffee and piece of bread. Already Peter had the horse harnessed to the chaise.

The day was cloudy. A fine rain fell. Yesterday there had been rain, too. Perhaps the drought was breaking. The doctor looked up at the sky with satisfaction. Any change in this August weather might help to check further spread of the disease.

The yellow fever, as he had so much feared, had suddenly taken an alarming turn. The day before a number of cases were reported from parts of the city other than the original Water Street neighborhood. On his advice, many of Rush's patients had already left town. The mayor of Philadelphia ordered that the filthy streets be cleaned up, an ineffectual order as it turned out afterward. Pennsylvania's Governor Thomas Mifflin was concerned, too. He ordered the port physician, Dr. James Hutchinson, to make a survey to determine whether an epidemic actually

43

did exist. Hutchinson doubted it very much, but he complied with the governor's request as far as to ask other doctors, including Rush, for their opinions on the question.

James Hutchinson was one of the Philadelphia physicians to hold an intense personal dislike for Rush. He could not easily bring himself to agree with Rush's warnings. It took three days for the port physician to convince himself that matters were serious, even under pressure of the governor's inquiry. This Sunday was the third day.

Usually Philadelphia slept late on Sunday morning. As Rush drove through the streets he noticed here and there unaccustomed activity. In front of some dwellings wagons and carriages were drawn up. Despite the rain, tight-faced men loaded baggage while children hung solemnly in the background. The great exodus from town had new vigor. Taking advantage of early daylight, families were leaving, some with specific places to go, others without destination at all. The wave of fear spread in earnest now.

As he passed, people shot suspicious glances at the doctor. They hurried faster with their preparations. They were not waiting to be *his* customers.

With increasing daylight a church bell rang out—*clang*—an interval—*clang*. The tolling bell for funerals. Even on Sunday. The dead could not wait.

On Water Street, Benjamin Rush tied up his horse and went into the house of the merchant and his son who were his patients. Farther down the street a hearse waited in front of another building. The doctor knocked at the door once, twice, then entered. The house was terribly silent. Suddenly fearful, the doctor hurried up the stairs. He had already noticed the almost overpowering stench in sickrooms of yellow-fever victims. He met it now. The bedroom doors were standing open. Rush went through the first, into the room where he had treated the man.

He saw at once that his patient was dead.

With a quick step he crossed to the bedside. The body was contorted as if the last moments were in horrible pain. At the end the man had thrown off his covering. The bed was soaked with black vomit and black liquid excrement and blood.

The doctor drew in his breath. He turned to go to the boy's room. There had not been a sound in the house. Yet standing in the second doorway he found the dazed mother.

"He's—dead," she mumbled.

"I know," Rush said. "I've seen. The boy—?"

"Both dead," the woman said.

The boy had died more tranquilly, almost with a little smile. But he had hemorrhaged from the mouth, ears, and bowels. Dr. Rush examined him briefly.

He was interrupted by a shrill cry from the mother. She remained in the doorway with an expression on her face showing that realization only now was coming to her. She held her hands to her face.

"Dead—both dead!" Her voice broke. With a choked moan she gasped, "Why? Why did they die? Why didn't you do something? Oh, Doctor, Dr. Rush—"

The doctor felt a suffocating constriction in his breathing. He must not give in to sympathy for his patients and their families. Otherwise he would sink under the loads of misery he must see. He glanced back again at the dead boy. The skin was turning black.

"I will send help to you," he told the woman. He saw she still wore her nightdress. "Best you get your clothes on."

"You're not leaving—you can't leave me—"

45

"I have other calls to make, madam." He said it as gently as he could.

On the street the doctor drew a deep breath at last. He knew the contagion was all over himself. He listened for a moment. Three bells tolled now in different parts of the city. One could be Christ Church, another probably the Presbyterian Church, and then one farther away St. Mary's Roman Catholic Church. Someone had started a huge fire a short distance up Water Street, and clouds of acrid smoke filled the air. Word had passed around that smoke might check the contagion.

Rush remembered histories he had read of plagues in Europe. Here were the scenes re-enacted. Only this was real, this was now, not pictures brought up by words on a printed page.

A second hearse came slowly along Water Street from Arch. Three Negro men were with it. The doctor interrupted their progress. He sent two of the men into the house of the newly widowed mother. All three had soaked their clothing in vinegar, and rain dripped from their hats.

"That be seven dead in this neighborhood since yesterday noon," the third man told him. "Heard o' four more last night at Kensington."

Kensington—that was the area beyond Callowhill Street, near the Northern Liberties. The disease still spread.

Rush untied his horse and drove off slowly in the chaise. The pathetic cries of the grieving woman haunted him. *Why didn't you do something, Dr. Rush? Why did they die?*

This fever mocked the power of medicine. He reviewed in his mind the treatment he had given each of his two patients: bark, quinine, spirits, blisters on the limbs, neck, and head to reduce the fever, a gentle purge

46

of calomel and ipecacuanha to induce a mild vomiting. Several previous cases had responded to temperate bleeding and small successive doses of physic. But then others had not.

How inadequate was knowledge! *Why didn't you do something, Dr. Rush?*

The bells continued tolling. Amid their clanging came sporadic sounds of musket fire as frightened householders discharged gunpowder to cleanse the air. Through the streets fires blazed high giving off clouds of smoke that lay low over the town and at the same time endangered even in today's drizzle every building in the city after the long spell of dry weather.

Philadelphia had come face to face with the most terrible tragedy of its hundred-and-ten-year history. Not war or occupation, threats of Indians, or previous epidemics could compare with what Dr. Rush foresaw for the weeks ahead. Death would sweep through the city careless of men or mothers, children, or aged, while the power and knowledge of medicine must stand by to watch.

7  *Rain on Sunday*

BY AFTERNOON of that Sunday in August the rain turned to a downpour and then to a near cloudburst. Under dark skies the streets ran in floods. Mud holes and swamps were filled, and so were water barrels. In the meteorological records for the day, this was called the "great rain." It would be the last rainfall of any consequence for more than seven weeks, until October 15.

All through the day reports of more sick persons kept coming in. More on Water Street, and others in still different city areas. Through the storm all day long processions of wagons, carts, and carriages moved along muddy roads leading to the country. Literally, thousands were fleeing. The city began to feel the effects of the unknown terror.

That afternoon Philadelphia's College of Physicians met in special session to consider the emergency, at the urgent request of Pennsylvania's Governor Mifflin. They gathered at their headquarters in a room of the American Philosophical Society building on the Fifth Street side of the square behind the State House—Independence Square. The College of Physicians had been established in 1787 with Benjamin Rush as one of the twelve founding Fellows. Its president was the same venerable Dr. John Redman under whom Rush had served his student apprenticeship.

Not all the College members thought the situation important enough to justify their facing the heavy rain. Most of those who did come to the meeting questioned the kind of disease that was killing Philadelphia's citizens. Few of them were ready to accept Benjamin Rush's diagnosis.

Besides Rush himself, among the physicians at the meeting were several of his closest friends. One was Dr. Samuel Powel Griffitts, Quaker and professor at the University of Pennsylvania. Another was young Caspar Wistar, also a founding member of the College of Physicians. A third was Dr. William Currie, an older man who had served as surgeon in the Revolution, a self-trained doctor, and another of the twelve founding Fellows.

Dr. William Shippen attended the meeting, too—the same Shippen with whom Rush had fought over the condition of army hospitals during the Revolution. With him was Adam Kuhn, a long-time practitioner in Philadelphia and a close associate of Shippen. These two sided together as the core of the old-school, conservative faction of Philadelphia's medical profession. Lined up with them was Hutchinson, port physician.

48

Potential friction was instantly apparent as the doctors gathered. Dr. Shippen and Dr. Rush merely nodded formally to each other. Kuhn was suspicious of Rush. So was Hutchinson. But Rush promptly dominated the College meeting. He felt the city's danger so deeply he would not be turned aside. Using his oratorical powers of persuasion to the fullest, he tried to convince his colleagues.

The arguments turned out not to be so much on the disease's deadliness as about its nature. Exactly what it was, and what medicines should be used to cope with it, were matters of individual opinion. Another disagreement was on origin. Rush claimed the disease was the yellow fever, and that it originated locally out of the filth in and around the city. The other faction disputed his theory, believing most of the sick were ill with common non-infectious fall fever, or if some cases were infectious, then their contagion was imported from the West Indies.

The conference was grave. Adam Kuhn disagreed with Rush on every point. Shippen glared. Griffitts supported Rush.

The controversy between Philadelphia's doctors crystallized at that moment. At issue were the two points—yellow fever's nature and origin—which remained contentious for years afterward. This meeting of the medical minds of the city marked the beginning of the great debate on the fever which was to split the profession asunder.

Rush made his views prevail for the moment. The meeting appointed a committee, which in turn nominated Rush himself to draw up a list of suggestions for the city's inhabitants to follow. The doctors adjourned until the following day. Rush hurried home through the storm-darkened streets to carry out the assignment. Here, he felt, was concerted action.

In his study that evening, Dr. Rush wrote down a list of points which seemed to him practical and effective. He suggested that people avoid all unnecessary contact with

49

persons infected, that doors and windows of houses containing infected persons be marked, that sick be placed in large and airy rooms with great attention paid to cleanliness of body and bed linen. Offensive matter should be removed from sickrooms as speedily as possible. He suggested a special hospital to be established for the poor. Remembering the gloominess of the tolling bells, he asked for a stop to the practice. Thinking of the city's morale, he believed funerals should be as unobtrusive as possible. Especially, he emphasized, streets and wharves should be kept clean.

He advised persons still well to take special care, noting that contagion could be taken into the body and pass out of it without producing the fever unless there was special reason induced by the condition of the individual infected. Avoid fatigue, he instructed—keep out of the sun, evening air, and drafts, be careful of dress, avoid intemperance.

His final suggestion called for elimination of the dangerous street fires, which he thought were ineffectual anyhow. He did recommend burning gunpowder, and he described the benefits of vinegar and camphor when used on handkerchiefs or in smelling bottles by those attending the sick.

The next day the College of Physicians unanimously adopted his recommendations. None of the other physicians had more constructive comments to offer. The list was promptly published in the newspapers.

Benjamin Rush was in a fair way to assume leadership of Philadelphia's fight against the great epidemic.

But the shadow of Dr. Shippen lay long in Rush's path.

The enmity between William Shippen and Benjamin Rush could scarcely have run deeper. Their Revolutionary War quarrel was one cause. Rush held Shippen personally responsible for the appalling hospital conditions which, he said, had led to the deaths of thousands of soldiers. During the war he had gone over Shippen's head to complain directly to General Washington. He expressed his views on Shippen publicly, in an open letter published in the newspapers.

Shippen, toward the end of the war, had actually been court-martialed for misconduct in his command. He was acquitted by a narrow margin, but the court did find that he had speculated in hospital stores for his own benefit, which conduct the judges considered "highly improper and justly reprehensible." At the trial Dr. Rush was a willing witness against Shippen.

Yet these war affairs had done little more than to harden a natural dislike of the two men for each other. They were opposites in personality—Rush outgiving, headstrong, progressive to the point of rashness, and Shippen autocratic, cautious, conservative. They disagreed utterly on matters professional.

Shippen's career had been a confusing mixture of brilliance and inadequacy. Shippen, Rush's senior in the profession, had wealth, social prestige, and influence. The Shippen family in its various branches was one of the most respected in Philadelphia. Dr. Shippen, like Rush, had been to Princeton and Scotland. He had conducted the first class in anatomy in Philadelphia, using dissections. Rush, then a student apprentice, attended.

That first anatomical course caused great excitement in Philadelphia. The story spread that Shippen was robbing graves for his dissection specimens. Aroused inhabitants attacked his house with stones. Hastily he announced that he was using bodies of suicides and executed criminals—only now and then one from potter's field. The body of a man executed in Gloucester, New Jersey, was

51

sent by court order to Dr. Shippen. So was a Negro who had committed suicide by cutting his throat with a glass bottle.

But when Benjamin Rush returned from Scotland a doctor in his own right, he found most of the older physicians in Philadelphia entrenched in their old-school theories. Rush had discovered in Edinburgh a new spirit in medicine, trying to shake off handicaps left over from the Dark Ages. He learned new ideas and practices, and enthusiastically brought them to America.

At that time medical knowledge was beginning to move forward after having drifted for centuries through mysticism, astrology, and superstition. Hipprocrates and the medical scholars of ancient Greece worked out theories of four humors in the human body: blood, phlegm, yellow bile or "choler," and black bile or "melancholy." The humors corresponded to the four elements: air (hot and moist like blood), water (cold and moist like phlegm), fire (hot and dry like choler), and earth (cold and dry like melancholy).

On these same theories hung the entire medical philosophy for hundreds of years, however extensively later physicians, theologians, and philosophers superimposed their own interpretations on them. Some of these interpretations of illness and treatment were constructive, others bordered on witchcraft.

Shortly after 1700 a Dutch physician named Boerhaave developed his own new system, that health was a balance of solids and fluids in the body. Disturbance of the balance resulted in disease. Maladjustments in solids came through changes in size, number, or placement of tissues. Fluids caused trouble by becoming sour, sharp, salty, aromatic, fatty, alkaline, or viscous. In reality these classifications were a new interpretation of the famed "humors" of the Hippocratic school and the Middle Ages.

Boerhaave gained fame also as a teacher. Students

from Europe, England, and America came to the university to study his system. Boerhaave developed the clinical method of teaching. On daily hospital rounds accompanied by pupils he reviewed the physical condition of each patient, took temperatures with a thermometer, examined urine and excretions with a hand lens.

The doctors of Philadelphia followed Boerhaave's theory of body chemistry and physical changes, and practiced his teaching of conservative use of medicine, diet, and profuse sweating. Dr. Redman, Rush's master, had studied at Leiden, so Benjamin Rush's apprenticeship was governed by these old traditions.

At Edinburgh, Rush found something quite different. Dr. William Cullen was developing new ideas, particularly that the nervous system was the key to life. Disease affected the nervous system, he claimed, either by making it too strong and putting it into a spasm, or weakening it into a state he called atony. Some fevers were spasms. Others, particularly typhus, were atony. Spasms were treated by depressants, atony by stimulants.

Benjamin Rush began practice in Philadelphia by endorsing Cullen's Edinburgh theories, in direct opposition to the established doctors who were Boerhaave adherents. He managed to get himself appointed professor of chemistry at the College of Philadelphia—the first man in America to gain the title. From this vantage point he lectured on the merits of Dr. Cullen's system. In effect, he told the older doctors of the city just how out of date they were. Cullen's system was built on the ruins of Boerhaave's, Rush cried. On one occasion he gave a toast before a number of students to "Speedy interment of the system of Dr. Boerhaave, and may it never rise again!" Another doctor overheard him. His words leaked back to the rest of the profession. Rush, the young upstart, was in trouble at once.

His ideas were too radical for most of the other physicians, even those who had themselves studied in Edinburgh in earlier years. The old-school members of the profession naturally resented the impudence of the young man preaching to them. One of these was Dr. William Shippen, by this time a settled physician of high reputation.

Rush himself admitted that perhaps the opposition to him was his own fault, by the manner in which he recommended the Cullen system. For the first seven years of his practice in Philadelphia, not one patient was sent to him by another doctor.

As early as this the newspaper war against him commenced. Articles appeared, anonymously, ridiculing the Cullen system and connecting Rush's name with it. The practice of writing anonymous newspaper pieces was common at the time. Benjamin Franklin used it to promote his own political projects, even to answering his own propositions with arguments for and against, all anonymously. The practice was supported by the principle of freedom of the press.

Dr. Rush replied in kind to attacks against him. He was blunt, self-opinionated, born with little tact or humor. He snapped back angrily at each rebuff. It followed that his path was hard, especially at the beginning. When he set up his own practice he had no backing, no name, no influence to help him. One man questioned whether his title meant doctor of physic or doctor of religion.

Rush earned his reputation slowly, step by step, through his own efforts despite the profession's resistance. He took care of the poor, visiting every alley in the city, walking into the distant country for lack of a horse, climbing ladders to upper stories of miserable huts, sitting on the beds of the sick when there were no chairs, becoming infected with vermin. When help was lacking, he administered his own prescriptions, bleeding, and clysters—the term for enemas. His office became crowded with the poor, and he supplied medicines from his own shop, as he called it, without charge. His income was meager, but he felt his reward lay in his actions. Leaving sickrooms, he repeated to himself a thousand times, *"Take care of him, and I will repay."*

People liked his reliance on fewer medicines than other doctors used. In London he had learned the new technique of smallpox inoculation. Instead of injecting the pus of the infection into a long incision in the arm, the new method called for the use of serum from an early blister of the disease through a small arm puncture. Patients came to Rush for this popular kind of inoculation and stayed with him for treatment of other ills. Word of his cures spread around the city.

He had finally gained a firm reputation not only in Philadelphia, but throughout the country. His students from other states carried his ideas back home with them. His publications on medical subjects were read as far away as Europe.

Yet the core of older Philadelphia doctors surrounding Shippen never accepted the presumptuous Rush. He was too zealous, too rebellious for their conservative ways. They endured his presence in the city but would not endorse him.

## 8    *"Heaven Alone Bore Witness"*

ON MONDAY morning five more persons died on Water Street, and many more all over the city became ill. The rainstorm had meant nothing. Schools closed or ceased to function because the students had fled to the country. Business activities slowed down. All usual affairs became overshadowed by the terrible uncertainty.

55

Tuesday Dr. Rush was called from bed at five-thirty in the morning. The disease built up strength. Townspeople, in state of shock, responded with apathy. On this day Rush sent off his two eldest boys to their mother in Princeton. The child Ben two days later went to relatives in the country near Philadelphia. His sister helped Rush to establish his house on an emergency basis. Already a stream of people calling at the house taxed facilities.

All the remedies Rush could think of failed. Bark, wine, and blisters made no impression. He tried wrapping patients in blankets soaked with warm vinegar. With one patient at least this treatment seemed to offer promise. He rubbed mercury ointment on the right side of other patients to stimulate circulation. Of thirteen persons treated by these means, only three recovered. The doctor decided they would have recovered anyway, perhaps sooner without the treatment.

He learned that a physician from the West Indies was in Philadelphia. This was Dr. Edward Stevens, a close friend of Alexander Hamilton, Secretary of the Treasury. Stevens had recently come from St. Croix. Rush thought he must have had experience with yellow fever. He called on Dr. Stevens for suggestions. He found the doctor cooperative, quite willing to advise. Long ago, Stevens said, he had found purges of all kinds to be harmful in treating yellow fever. The disease yielded more readily to bark, wine, and especially to cold baths. It was best to administer bark not only by mouth but also by way of clysters, rectal injections. Baths, he emphasized, should be administered by throwing buckets of cold water over the naked body. To Rush the advice seemed reasonable. Other physicians in Philadelphia were using similar methods. One writer had said that bark injections were useful when the bowels were full of vicious humors.

Rush began the suggested remedies the next day. At

56

first he had great confidence in their success. He prescribed bark in large quantities, in one case to be injected into the bowels every four hours. He directed that buckets of cold water be thrown frequently over his patients.

But of four persons so treated, three died. That was enough proof of Dr. Stevens' theories for Rush.

He exchanged ideas with his friend Dr. Caspar Wistar. Yet so far there seemed to be only one preventive —to flee from the city. And no remedy at all.

He was desperate. "Heaven alone bore witness to the anguish of my soul in this awful situation," he said of this time. Everything at his command was ineffectual, and his patients as well as those of other doctors were dying. There was no standing in the way of this disease. Nothing in the country's history has been known to equal the epidemic.

The fever struck in different ways. Sometimes it came on with chills and high fever, but more often with headache, languor, and sick stomach. The symptoms were followed by stupor, delirium, vomiting, dry skin, cold hands and feet, feeble pulse. The eyes, at first diffused with blood, became yellow. By the third or fourth day the whole skin often turned yellow. Most persons died on the second or third day, and few survived the fifth day of fever. Toward the end, the body showed livid spots, there was bleeding, and vomiting of black matter.

Rush referred again to his 1762 apprentice's notebook. In that year the fever had also started in August. With horror Rush found it had continued even into December. The deaths then of twenty persons a day were already being exceeded now, and this was not yet the end of August. He guessed what must lie ahead.

He was fully aware of the danger to himself. "Another night and morning has been added to my life," he wrote to Julia. He begged her, "Help me, dear Julia, by your prayers to be always ready. I have cut out much work for my Divine Master to be performed in months or years to come, but if He means to have it completed by other hands, 'His will be done'!"

A long, agonizing struggle lay ahead if his life was spared. His sister placed a mattress across chairs in the back room of the house so he could lie down for brief rests when he returned from calls. Rebecca and their mother both helped prepare medicines and took care of the patients now coming to the house by scores for treatment.

Rush had four apprentices with him at this time. He brought one of them, a nineteen-year-old boy named Johnny Stall, into the house to live temporarily, to provide one more pair of hands.

Still the people died.

By the last week in August Rush was goaded beyond endurance by his uselessness. He spent long night hours vainly searching through his library books for some clue. Each one contradicted the other. While he read desperately, he could hear the rattle of wheels through the dark streets as solitary corpses were carried past on chair shafts on their lonely way to the graveyards. Few mourners followed them, or none. The doctor feared this was only the beginning. In his vision he saw prospects of the near and perhaps total destruction of his city.

One night was the grimmest of all. Rush had taken to sitting in a corner of his front room, in darkness and silence, trying to think of some way to approach the baffling terror of this disease. He wrung his hands and literally wept. "Oh, that the hand of the Lord may be with me," he cried aloud, "not only to preserve my life but to heal my poor patients!"

In this ultimate despair he went over every experience in his life, everything he had learned. Holding his head in his hands in the dark room, he thought of the men who had taught him, the ones whose works he had read. He thought of Cullen, and Sydenham, an earlier English doctor who had dissolved much medical superstition, and of the learned doctors of London. He remembered conversations with physicians, philosophers—Franklin quoting the famous Dr. Joseph Priestley of England, and others.

All his professional life Rush had searched for new ways to combat illness. He had learned well, in medicine as well as politics, Bostock's lesson in Edinburgh that no man's claims should be accepted at face value as truth. One had to find one's own personal conviction. And always new truths lay just over the horizon.

Never satisfied, forever seeking, his interest in experimenting went back to his university days. The experiment he used for his graduation thesis astonished the staid University of Edinburgh. His subject was digestion in the stomach. To determine the effect of fermentation he made a firsthand test on himself. He took five grains of alkaline salt to destroy any acidity in his own stomach, and then ate a full and carefully cooked dinner of beef, cheese, bread, and beer. After three hours he swallowed two grains of emetic tartar and threw up the whole. The resulting disgorgement was carefully studied for acidity. He repeated the test a second time, using veal instead of beef and water instead of beer. Still a third time he did the same thing. His last menu was chicken, cabbage, and unleavened bread. The resulting findings, that digestion was aided by natural stomach acids, were incorporated into his thesis, written in classical Latin and dedicated to, among others, Benjamin Franklin.

Although Rush's early practice in Philadelphia was based so strongly on the Cullen theories, as years went by he became dissatisfied with them. The Edinburgh system, he discovered, contained errors. For a man of Rush's integrity it was a shattering experience to doubt the principles for which he himself had struggled. He passed through a period of discouragement. If he had to doubt his own preceptor, Cullen, then where was truth?

By the time this happened, the other Philadelphia physicians had adopted Cullen's system. They no longer followed Boerhaave. Rush might have rested there, avoiding further conflict with his colleagues. Most of them accepted the now-current methods as entirely adequate. What else could be learned, they asked. Cullen's reputation worked against him every time Rush mentioned an idea that ran counter to the Cullen system. As always, the rebelling Rush was tortured on the rack of status quo.

He could not accept that position. He went on for a time using partly theory, partly cut-and-try methods. He read, and thought, and observed diseases without discovering anything that satisfied him.

He was appointed professor of theory and practice of physic in the school shortly to be merged with the University of Pennsylvania. He had to give his students a system of medical principles in which he himself believed. One night as he paced the floor of his study, he thought of it. A whole series of ideas came to him, each one fitting perfectly with the others. The result was practically an entirely new system of medicine, based not on Cullen or past teachers and writers, but on Rush himself.

The leading principle of his system was that diseases were caused by "debility," or weakness and languor in the human body. It was the principle for which Rush ultimately became famous. Debility must come either directly, from lack of "stimulation" in the body, or indirectly from too much stimulation. Sudden debility brought about a "morbid excitement" in the blood vessels resulting in fever. Chronic debility lessened blood vessel "excitement."

60

These assumptions were opposed to Cullen's teaching of spasms and atony in the nervous system. Rush was in the thick of another fight. But at last he had arrived at his own system, not with an intent to do so as an end in itself, but rather because his thirsting mind sought for new truths.

Something of the same kind happened that dark night of the yellow-fever epidemic. Nothing that Rush had ever devised before could match the power of the disease. As he sat in his room thinking of every theory he had learned, every experience that might help, the name of Franklin kept recurring.

Benjamin Franklin—he tried to remember. Then it came to him. Of course, shortly before his death Franklin had given him an old manuscript from his collection. Written years before, it had something to do with yellow fever. Once the paper had been read before the American Philosophical Society.

It was the thinnest hope, but Rush jumped from his chair, hurried to light a candle. He almost ran to his collection of old records and papers accumulated through the years. Fingers trembling, he sought the manuscript, found it. He took it to a table and by the flickering candlelight read it through.

The paper had been written by a Dr. John Mitchell half a century before. It contained a report on yellow fever in Virginia, in 1741. Rush's eye caught certain passages on purges. The manuscript stated that purges were more necessary in this disease than in others. They produced gentle sweats which helped and sometimes nipped the fever in the bud. All putrid fevers required some evacuation to bring them to a perfect crisis and solution.

All at once came a dramatic moment. Benjamin Rush told his own story of reading that manuscript:

"Here I paused. A new train of ideas suddenly broke

61

in upon my mind. I believed the weak and low pulses which I had observed in this fever to be the effect of debility of the *indirect* kind"—meaning from *overstimulation* of the body by poisonous matters—"but the unsuccessful issue of purging and even of a spontaneous diarrhea in a patient of Dr. Hutchinson's had led me not only to doubt of, but to dread, its effects. My fears from this evacuation were confirmed by the communications I had received from Dr. Stevens. I had been accustomed to raising a weak and low pulse in pneumony and apoplexy by means of bloodletting, but I had attended less to the effects of purging in producing this change in the pulse. Dr. Mitchell in a moment dissipated my ignorance and fears upon the subject."

To reduce overexcitement in the blood vessels, Rush's treatment was bleeding. Now Dr. Mitchell's manuscript on yellow fever suggested the possibility of purges for the same effect.

Rush had found a key. To oppose the yellow fever, he could *induce* debility instead of counteracting it. Why had he not thought of this before, he wondered. In a sense it meant an extension of his previous theories. Yet the drastic extreme of inducing debility was new. To take a patient already weak with fever and weaken him still further seemed fantastic at first.

But to weaken the body's "overstimulation" that was causing the fever itself made sense to him.

This was no time to be hesitant. The enemy to be fought was massive and implacable. This kind of enemy would give in to nothing but the strongest countermeasures.

It remained now, Rush thought, only to fix upon a suitable purge.

His memory helped again. During the War of Independence he had seen one Dr. Thomas Young, a surgeon in army hospitals, giving a purge of calomel in combination with jalap. The latter was a purgative powder made from the root of a Mexican plant. Calomel, derivative of mercury, had been used in the past by Rush, and had been recommended by a number of leading practitioners.

The dose used by the army surgeon was ten grains of calomel to ten of jalap. The jalap hastened action, for calomel was slow. At the time of the war Rush expressed astonishment at the strength of the purge, but later became convinced of its safety. It was known in wartime by the simple name of "ten and ten."

Dr. Rush thought long and hard through that night. He thought again in the morning.

The date was August 30. On his first call he saw a man who the day before had been almost dead. The patient was a blockmaker named Richard Spain, who lived on Third Street. Rush took along his young apprentice, Johnny Stall. As they approached the house a neighbor intercepted them.

"Dr. Rush, about Mr. Spain—"

"He still lives?"

"Yes, but that's the point. I feel it is my duty, Doctor, to say you ought to warn the family to make the funeral arrangements. They have given up hope, but await your word."

"We'll see," the doctor replied curtly.

He found the patient in a cold sweat. For twelve hours now his pulse had been too weak to feel. Rush made his decision. He gave Spain the purging dose, full strength.

Then he turned to Johnny Stall. "You will watch the patient. Repeat the dose three or four times today, until it operates."

During that day Dr. Rush gave the purge to four other patients, several of them far advanced with fever.

That evening Johnny reported back, "It operated!
63

Mr. Spain's pulse rose immediately, and a warm perspiration succeeded the cold sweat!"

"Then continue tomorrow," Rush said swiftly.

Richard Spain received purge doses on August 31 and September 1, until he had taken a total of eighty grains of calomel and somewhat more than that of jalap and rhubarb. The sick man revived. He was shortly out of danger, survived the epidemic, and lived afterward in good health.

Of the four other patients to whom Rush gave the medicine that first day, three were cured.

## 9  The Giant Refreshed by Wine

ON TUESDAY, September 3, the miracle happened. Blessed be God, Rush exclaimed, of twelve persons to whom he had been called the day before, eight were out of danger. One boy, in feverish delirium only last evening, was out of bed and downstairs. All had taken the powerful new medicine.

Two others died, both being cases to which Rush had been called in consultation. One was the sixth victim in the patient's family.

That night Benjamin Rush wrote jubilantly to a Trenton doctor to inform him of the great discovery. At last he had arrested the fever's fatality, he said. Calomel was responsible. "The patient should drink plentifully of chicken water or water gruel and lie in bed during the operation of the physic for it generally sweats as copiously as it purges." He explained the reason for the treatment. "From dissections it appears that the liver is either inflamed or obstructed, and the bile much vitiated in the gall bladder or in the small bowels. The calomel expels the latter and opens the obstructions of the former." He
64

said that this method of treating the disease had saved nine out of ten when applied in the early stages.

But he quickly discovered that "ten and ten" was not strong enough. Rush made the prescription ten grains of calomel and fifteen of jalap, a dose to be given three times, six hours apart.

On Wednesday the fever in the city was spreading but the mortality lessened. Again for Rush the mercury and jalap were curing nine out of ten patients.

On Thursday, Dr. Rush visited and prescribed for nearly one hundred persons. The mercury kept mortality to that of common bilious fever. He was saving twenty-nine out of every thirty patients to whom he was called on the first day of illness. He had not lost a single patient for two nights. The vital importance of the purge, he emphasized, was that it be given at the start of the disease.

By Friday evening Rush wrote to Julia, "The new medicine bears down nearly all opposition. Out of one hundred persons who have taken it from me *on the first day,* not one has died."

He thought he had a preventive, too, as well as a cure. It consisted, not in drenching the stomach with wine, bark, and bitters as other doctors prescribed, but in keeping the bowels gently open, for in them the disease first fixed its poison.

Yet the fever still raged in Philadelphia, sweeping ever upward. More and more inhabitants became infected with it, and the funerals went on. The sickness began to strike down the physicians themselves. Dr. Hutchinson became ill after dining with Thomas Jefferson at the latter's country home at Gray's Ferry on the Schuylkill. Dr. Wistar was stricken, Dr. Kuhn was ill. The burden increased on those remaining.

Rush had lost no time in advising the other doctors of his discovery. On Tuesday the third he gave the prescription to the College of Physicians. Undoubtedly every medical man in Philadelphia knew immediately what Rush was doing, and of the results he claimed.

What was happening?

In his letter to the Trenton doctor Rush had said in a postscript, "Some of our physicians condemn the above practice, but it is only those who have seen little of the disease. Those who have seen most of it have adopted it." That was on the very day he reported his news to the College.

About the same time he heard of Dr. Hutchinson's illness. He hurried at once to see the port physician. Take the new medicine, he urged. The doctor on his sickbed refused. Already he was under the care of two younger physicians. They supported Hutchinson's obstinacy, rejecting Rush's suggestion. On Thursday evening Hutchinson died. "Poor fellow!" Rush wrote Julia. "He died as well as lived my enemy." He thought of the time Hutchinson had denied the existence of a contagious fever after it appeared. "The reason, I fear," Rush said, "was the first account of it came *from me*."

Dr. Wistar, when he fell ill, took the medicine. He recovered. Dr. Kuhn recovered, but probably without the benefit of Rush's "ten and ten."

For Benjamin Rush, with his new method, found himself running headlong into a phalanx of opposition. To purge so drastically broke all precedents. Most physicians agreed that mild treatments, such as those suggested by Dr. Stevens from the West Indies, were the only properly effective ones.

At first Rush was surprised. Then he became caustic. At last he was thoroughly enraged. They were ignorant and stupid, he cried.

Dr. Griffitts adopted Rush's method, and so did a few

others. But the Shippen-Kuhn faction scoffed at Benjamin Rush.

On Saturday, September 7, a fire swept Philadelphia's water front. Rush thought the exertion of fire fighting weakened many men who subsequently caught the fever. On Sunday Rush wrote to his wife, "The disease has awakened like a giant refreshed by wine. I have this day been called to more new cases than I have time to count."

Two more doctors fell sick, another died. Then Alexander Hamilton became ill. His physician was his friend, the same Dr. Stevens. Grief and worry in the city were becoming too universal to matter any more. Yet still Rush could say that ninety-nine out of every hundred who took his mercury and jalap on the first day recovered.

The fever appeared to him to take a more virulent form. He decided he could go a step further in his treatment. If debilitation of the body by purging was effective, he could do more to ensure the results. He recorded afterward, "I did not rely upon purging alone to cure the disease. The theory of its proximate cause which I adopted led me to use other remedies to abstract excess of stimulus from the system."

If he could induce debility by massive purging, he decided he could intensify the result by bleeding.

He left home on the morning of September 8 with this cautious thought in mind.

The doctor had to make a call at the Pennsylvania Hospital. He drove his carriage up Walnut Street, passing potter's field on the left between Sixth and Seventh streets. Gravediggers were at work, stoically shoveling while new coffins arrived on chaise shafts. The gravediggers had set up crude tents so they could live at the scene of their work. The tents were placed around now-forgotten trenches

67

filled with several thousand bodies of Revolutionary War soldiers who had died in hospitals.

Rush turned his head away and spoke sharply to his horse.

Preoccupied as he reached Eighth Street and turned south toward the hospital, he did not notice the small boy darting through a gate and running to head him off.

"Doctor! Doctor—"

*Clippety-clop* . . .

The boy reached the carriage and ran along beside it. He was without a jacket and his hair was tousled.

"Hold here, whoa." The doctor pulled on the reins and the horse slowed.

"We have a sick man, my mother sent me for you, she saw you driving along the road. Please come to our house."

Dr. Rush looked down at the boy. He did not know him. The horse continued at a walk while the boy stepped quickly to keep up.

"What is this now?" the doctor said. "I have too many calls to make this morning."

"It's one of our boarders, he's awfully sick, a sailor from a ship. Mother says please to come, he's near to die."

"I'm on my way to the hospital. This is a busy day. Where is your house?"

"Back there, the gray one with the fence. You know us, Doctor—"

His frown increasing, Dr. Rush turned his head. With difficulty he peered around the high collar of his coat. He did remember the house. The woman had lost her husband early in the epidemic. He was called in, but not until the third day when it was too late. He remembered that the woman took in boarders.

"Mother says please come—"

"Hmm."

68

The doctor stared at the boy again. Then he jumped from the carriage and threw the reins to the boy.

"Hitch up the horse, please, and save me time. Make sure you tie the lines well."

"Yes, sir." The boy moved with alacrity. He watched the doctor walk back quickly to the house behind the fence.

The door opened before Dr. Rush raised his hand to knock. The woman was there, face sullen and drawn.

"It's the new boarder, came four days ago," she commenced without preliminaries. "He's off a ship. I don't want him dyin' in my house, Doctor. I got my place to think of."

"Where is he?"

"The upstairs back bedroom. I been up 'most all night."

"Take me to him."

She moved up the stairs, the battered slippers on her feet slapping the boards. The whole house looked as slovenly as she herself, but the doctor was accustomed to such calls. The air on the second floor was humid and close, even more so in the room where the sick man lay.

The woman paused at the door and inclined her head without a word. The doctor entered. He saw a gaunt form stretched on a narrow cot, the body covered with blankets so that only the face showed, thin and twisted with burning black eyes. A mass of uncombed hair clung to the pillowless sheet. The man's mouth opened and he breathed with difficulty. His lips twitched. He was sick indeed, and the room smelled of his sickness.

Dr. Rush pulled a wooden chair to the bedside and sat down, smiling cheerfully. "When did this start?" he asked.

The man's face moved.

"He won't answer you," the woman said, coming unwillingly into the room. "He complained yesterday morning. By last night he was took bad."

"Why didn't you call a doctor sooner?"

" 'Tain't my business about my boarders," she flared. "What am I? I just want none of 'em dyin' here."

Rush reached for the man's arms to take the pulse. Under the blanket the thin body burned. Checking carefully by both wrists, the doctor found the patient's pulse high, jumping intermittently.

"A cup of water and spoon," he ordered quickly. The landlady left. Rush had with him already-prepared doses of calomel and jalap. As soon as the woman returned he stirred the powders in the cup and made the patient drink.

"Now bring me a basin, and clean towels and hot water."

While the woman was gone this time, the doctor took a bandage from his pocket. Carefully he applied it to the patient's upper arm, not too tightly. Attentively he studied the man's face. His eyes were closed now but his open mouth showed the telltale red brightness with the early suspicion of a black streak. His eyes had a yellowish cast. Half-uttered sounds came from him, not words but strangled groans.

The woman brought back the articles Rush ordered. He reached into his waistcoat pocket for a small wooden case. He opened it and removed a rectangular metal object. It had a razor-sharp oval blade protruding from one end, and a spring catch on its side. He took the patient's bare right arm, and placed it, point of elbow turned down, over the basin which the landlady had brought. The fingers of the doctor's left hand felt again for the sick man's pulse. Then with his right hand Dr. Rush held the metal object over the median basilic vein in the crook of the elbow. He released the spring. With a little click the lancet blade plunged deeply through the skin and into the vein. A spurt of blood leaped out. The man's eyes opened and he

70

cried aloud. His arm jerked but the doctor's grasp was firm.

The woman standing beside the doctor made a slight sound. Dr. Rush deftly removed the blade, and allowed the pulsating stream to flow into the basin.

"Lie quietly," the doctor said. "I believe you will feel better."

The glazed eyes responded for a moment. The patient's tongue moved to moisten the dry lips. For a moment the state of delirium seemed to be gone. As the blood flowed the pulse beat under the doctor's fingers steadied a little, slowed down.

There was no sound in the room except for the soft dripping into the basin. The patient's face turned white, yet he lay still.

The pulse dropped slowly, but it must go further. The doctor's brows crinkled as the beat escaped him for a moment. More time passed, then—

Dr. Rush moved quickly, tightened and tied the bandage around the upper arm. With a moistened towel he wiped the skin clean. He took up the basin of blood, quickly judged the amount. He had taken approximately twelve ounces.

"I will send a bleeder, one of my students, to come this evening," he said to the landlady. "The bleeder will take an amount equal to this. I will ask you to repeat the purging medicine in six hours. I will leave the dose with you—"

The woman was hostile. "You better be sending a nurse, Dr. Rush," she said, "or get him to Bush Hill. I ain't got time or inclination—"

Bush Hill was the large manor house near the city taken over as a yellow-fever hospital for the poor. It was crowded already, and the doctors were ignoring Rush's recommendations on the purging medicine.

Rush's face reddened angrily. "You know how scarce

71

nurses are now," he snapped. "As for Bush Hill—would you murder this man? Remember, madam, works of mercy to the souls and bodies of men are means of grace."

He turned away from the woman. "You're in from a ship, I hear," he said to the patient. "You are English?"

The sick man tried to find his voice, then nodded.

"You'll be looking forward to being at sea again. You're in good hands here." The doctor paused, then added carefully, "You need not fear. You have nothing but a yellow fever."

He inclined his head to the man and left the room. Outside the door he stopped to speak to the landlady. "The less he eats in this stage the better," he told her. "If your boarder responds as previous cases of this disorder have under this manner of treatment, he should be cured in several days."

She stared at him. "If this be so— I thought he was like to die. Thanks to you for sparing me that."

"He will thank you, madam, but especially he should thank the goodness of God. You know the suggestions for avoiding the infection by yourself and your family?"

"Yes, sir, as 'twas in the newspaper."

Rush walked rapidly from the house. The fresh air was good again. The horse stood patiently, and Benjamin Rush climbed back into the carriage.

He tried bleeding another patient that day, tentatively and in the same small quantity. He became convinced that the method was good.

Then came September 10, a day Rush described as the most awful he had ever seen. Forty people were reported to have been buried that day. Rush himself visited and prescribed for more than one hundred patients.

The day following brought an even greater crisis. Once again Rush saw more than a hundred sick people. But for him it was a day of triumph. He reported joy fully to Julia that of the hundred he had visited, he had not a single death. "Thank God," he cried, "I have lost none."

"Never before," he said of his own feelings, "did I experience such sublime joy in contemplating the success of my remedies. It repaid me for all the toil and studies of my life. The conquest of this formidable disease was not the effect of accident nor the application of simple remedies, but it was the triumph of a principle in medicine."

But on September 11 an open letter to the Philadelphia public appeared in the Philadelphia *General Advertiser*. The writer was Dr. Adam Kuhn. He told the people that, with regard to the malignant fever, he did not prescribe emetics or laxatives unless normally required. He detailed a method of treatment by clyster injections of quinine bark and wine. He put the greatest dependence for curing the disease, he stated, on throwing cold water over the naked bodies of his patients. The latter treatment was refreshing, he said, and induced gentle sweats.

He cited Dr. Stevens as the authority on such procedure. Kuhn was following the methods of the West Indies practitioner.

Benjamin Rush replied instantly. He had his own open letter published the next day, September 12, in another paper. He regretted, he said in his letter, that he was unable to respond to all the calls on him by persons indisposed with the prevailing fever. He recommended that those unable to get medical aid take the mercurial purge themselves. He had arranged with the local apothecaries to supply the medicine. The purges should be followed by bloodletting to the extent of ten or twelve ounces if headache and fever continued. If purges could not be obtained or did not operate speedily, bleeding *now* (he emphasized this) could be used anyway. "The almost

73

universal success with which it hath pleased God to bless the remedies of strong mercurial purges and bleeding in this disorder enables Dr. Rush to assure his fellow citizens that there is no more danger to be apprehended from it, when those remedies are used in its early stages, than there is from the measles or influenza."

So the stricken and bewildered people of Philadelphia were told by each faction.

Rush also wrote a more specific letter to the College of Physicians. This letter was published, too. The usual weekly meetings of the College had been broken off, either because of expediency, lack of time, or general disagreement. His letter indicated the extent of the split among the profession. At least he wanted to pass along for the benefit of everyone else his own discoveries. "I have found bleeding to be useful, not only in cases when the pulse was full and quick but where it was *slow* and *tense*. I have bled in one case with the pulse beat only forty-eight strokes in a minute, and recovered my patient by it. The pulse becomes more full and frequent after it. This state of the pulse seems to arise from an inflamed state of the brain, which shows itself in a preternatural dilation of the pupils of the eyes. It is always unsafe to trust to the most perfect remissions of fever and pain in this state of the pulse. It indicates the necessity for more bleeding and purging. I have found it to occur most frequently in children."

He went on, "I have bled twice in many, and in one acute case four times, with the happiest effects. I consider intrepidity in the use of the lancet at the present time to be as necessary as is the use of mercury and jalap in this insidious and ferocious disease."

Rush's friend, Dr. William Currie, suddenly turned against him with a published letter which denied the existence in town of any extensive yellow fever. Most of the sickness, Currie said, was the common fall fever,

74

brought on by influenza. Though bloodletting was proper enough for that kind of fever, the doctor stated, in cases of true yellow fever Rush's recommendations would be fatal.

Then Rush's close friend Caspar Wistar, previously ill of the fever and cured—Rush believed—by the mercury purges, expressed public doubts on the method. To Rush this was an act of treachery. "The most unkindly cut of all," Rush cried bitterly.

But Dr. Griffitts had also caught the fever. Rush did have his defenders and among them Quaker Griffitts was one. Grateful for his recovery due to purging and blood-letting, he published his own testimonial: "If my poor frame, reduced by previous sickness, great anxiety and fatigue, and a very low diet, could bear *seven* bleedings in five days beside purging, and no diet but toast and water, what shall we say of physicians who bleed but once?"

Dr. Kuhn, after recovering from the fever, fled to Bethlehem, Pennsylvania, not to return until the epidemic was over. From afar he continued his letters through the press castigating Rush.

Dr. Shippen had disappeared at the beginning of the epidemic and, according to Rush, was "nobody knows where."

A crushing attack on Rush came from an unexpected quarter. This time a letter addressed to the College of Physicians was printed in every newspaper of the city. It was signed by Alexander Hamilton, Secretary of the Treasury.

Hamilton described his illness, how he had been cared for, and recovered. His doctor—Stevens. He proceeded with a testimonial to Dr. Stevens.

Following the testimonial, in the same publications, came a treatise by Stevens himself on the disease and its treatment. The West Indian physician took special care to condemn violent evacuations in a debilitating disease requiring stimulants—bark, wine, spirits.

It was a devastating repudiation of Dr. Rush, made not only by the well-known physician from the West Indies but supported both directly and indirectly by a major officer of the United States Government. Besides his official position, Hamilton was the leader of the Federalist party. Rush, a friend of Thomas Jefferson, was on the other side of the political fence.

Suddenly it seemed that politics had intruded into the battle against the epidemic.

For Alexander Hamilton to support the doctor who had brought him through the fever seemed natural. Could any other motive be suspected? Rush thought so. He said, "I think it probable that if the new remedies had been introduced by any other person than a decided Democrat and a friend of Madison and Jefferson, they would have met with less opposition from Colonel Hamilton."

It was not the first time Hamilton had been aware of Rush. During the War of Independence the colonel served as Washington's personal aide. He had been a close witness of the Rush-Shippen medical affair, after which General Washington more or less cautiously endorsed Shippen. Hamilton was also present when Governor Patrick Henry sent to Washington at his Valley Forge headquarters an anonymous letter of criticism which the commander in chief correctly guessed came from Dr. Rush.

That he ever wrote such a letter—the sense of which was that Washington ought to be removed from command —the doctor regretted ever afterward. He had not done it in any spirit of politics, but from a rash and ill-advised impulse brought on by American defeats in the war. Washington eventually forgave Rush, but nothing indicated that Hamilton forgot the subversive act on the part of the Philadelphia doctor.

76

By the year of the yellow fever, 1793, the Hamilton-Jefferson quarrel grew into an insoluble stalemate. Hamilton, Secretary of the Treasury, offered fiscal policies for the government which Jefferson opposed. Jefferson, as Secretary of State, leaned sympathetically in favor of the French Revolution, which Hamilton abhorred. So divided were the two men that Washington himself could not reconcile their differences, or their hatreds.

The rift in the Cabinet in Philadelphia spread over the country, dividing even further the Federalist faction and those who called themselves "Democrats," who came to be known as "Democratic-Republicans." Benjamin Rush, by disposition and belief, was on the Jeffersonian side. His opinions were not secret. Certainly Hamilton knew.

The circumstances closed in on the doctor. He was already in a political squeeze. Meanwhile, in his opinion, the lives of Philadelphians were at stake.

Rush charged that, by confusing the public on his new, efficient methods of treating yellow fever, "Colonel Hamilton's letter has cost our city several hundred inhabitants."

## 10    "In the Midst of Death I Am in Life"

BY THE second week of September, Dr. Rush was regularly caring for more than a hundred patients each day. By now he felt his own body to be full of contagion. His eyes and sometimes his skin turned yellow, his pulse beat fast. The nights were awful. Because of the frequent calls at his door, the doctor had little sleep. Through the dark hours he lay awake thinking about his family, his patients. He sweated profusely, sweats so offensive that he was forced to pull the bedclothes close around his neck. He gave up normal eating, relying for strength on weak broth, milk, potatoes, raisins, and coffee.

One night he felt alarmingly ill. Nevertheless, he rose as usual in the morning. Merely as a safeguard he had himself bled ten ounces. Then he went off in his chaise, and before midday dinner visited almost fifty patients.

At one house he was overcome by sudden weakness, and had to lie down for a few minutes. He forced himself on. His weary mind and exhausted body seemed like separate things now. This world of sickness and death was becoming dreamlike and unreal.

A friend was ill, a schoolmaster named Miles Mervin. Rush had cared for him at first, but the schoolmaster's friends persuaded him to change doctors, to dismiss his purging, bloodletting physician in favor of a Frenchman who relied instead on bark and wine. A number of refugee French doctors in town were objects of Rush's antipathy because they persisted in following Stevens' theories. On this particular day Mervin had called Rush back again.

Through days and weeks uncounted Benjamin Rush had seen such scenes of heartbreak that he thought he could no longer be moved. Yet of this case of Miles Mervin he said, "My mind was suddenly thrown off its pivots." As he entered the sickroom, Mervin moved his hands with pathetic pleading, gasping, "Doctor! Doctor, help me, good God, help me!"

Beyond all help the man was dying. His cries turned to screams. "Help—help!" His wife at the bedside was in a torment of her own emotions. Something snapped within the doctor. Though the identical kind of tragedy happened many times every day throughout the city, this last case was too much for Rush to bear. He knew Mervin too well, knew his goodness—

He fled from the house. It was awful. Oh, Kuhn,

78

Kuhn, Rush sobbed, if it had not been for your invidious publications that did such immense mischief, probably even the French doctors would have accepted the new treatments! As it was, scores of people like Miles Mervin were being sacrificed to the bark and wine treatment which Rush believed to be utterly ineffectual. Perhaps the new purging and bleeding methods could have eradicated the whole contagion from the city in a few weeks. But they, Rush thought, the doctors such as Kuhn and Stevens, not only refused to adopt his system, but persecuted and slandered its originator.

By two o'clock that afternoon, Rush came down with his own first attack of yellow fever.

He took a dose of the mercury medicine and went to bed. He took another dose in the evening, was bled ten more ounces. In the morning he bathed his face, hands, and feet in cold water, drank hyson tea and water in which currant jelly had been dissolved. By eight o'clock he felt well enough to confer with his apprentices and to receive patients in his room. To Julia he wrote, "In consequence of losing blood and taking one of my purges I am now perfectly well—so much so that I rested better last night than I have done for a week past. Thus you see that I have proved upon my own body that the yellow fever when treated in the new way is no more than the common cold."

The following morning he was downstairs again, and in his parlor prescribed for about one hundred persons during the day.

On the first day of Rush's illness there had been sixty-seven funerals in Philadelphia. Within the following week the number nearly doubled. The city was a shambles of desolation. "Don't think of coming to see me," Rush told Julia. "Our city is a great mass of contagion. The very air in it is now offensive to the smell . . . many die without

79

nurses. Some perish for want of a draft of water. Parents desert their children as soon as they are infected, and in every room you enter you see no person but a solitary black man or woman near the sick. Many people thrust their parents into the street as soon as they complain of a headache. Two such exiles have taken sanctuary for half a day in our kitchen."

In laconic technical prose Rush described the disease in the account he wrote of it. "The pain in the head was acute and distressing. It affected the eyeballs in a peculiar manner. A pain extended in some cases from the back of the head down the neck. The ears are affected in several persons with a painful sensation which they compared to a string drawing their two ears together through the brain. The sides, and the regions of the stomach, liver, and bowels were all, in different people, the seat of either dull or active pain. The stomach towards the close of the disorder was affected with burning or spasmodic pain of the most distressing nature. It produced cries and shrieks which were often heard on the opposite sides of the streets to where the patients lay."

Grim stories came out of the plague. An example was the case of a pregnant woman who, as her husband and two children died in the same room, went into labor. Her cries at the window brought up a carter employed by the committee for the relief of the sick. With his assistance she was delivered of a child which died in a few minutes. Almost immediately the mother died, too. In one room lay five dead bodies, one family annihilated by the fever in an hour or so.

There were not enough doctors, or nurses, or bleeders. There were not enough gravediggers. Wages of nurses climbed to three dollars and a half a day, then even higher.

In the crisis the Negroes of Philadelphia's new African Church rose to the fore as a band of heroes. They served as bleeders, nurses, caretakers for the poor, and in every conceivable capacity of assistance, in many cases contributing their work without pay. Rush testified to the courage of his friends, Billy Gray and Absalom Jones.

Rush was out on the streets again three days after his attack. He gave up driving his own chaise and hired a closed hack to take him on calls. The driver's name was Frederick. The fever left Rush with appalling weakness. Now he had to pull himself up stairways to patients' rooms by clinging to the banisters. In his pocket he carried a vial of wine, and if he felt faintness coming on he took a mouthful, holding it a few moments before spitting it out. For preserving strength, he would sit at patients' bedsides and drink milk and eat fruit. After all, he thought, no sickroom could be more contaminated than his own house after the hundreds who had come there for treatment.

They kept coming, mostly poor people who needed his advice. The doctor did not charge them for these services, or for the medicines he gave out. His sister aided in caring for the visitors. Rebecca was tireless in making up prescriptions. The apprentices were tireless, too, in carrying their share of the load. Johnny Stall, Edward Fisher, John Coxe who was old Dr. Redman's grandson, and Johnny Alston were their names. They were scarcely more than boys, yet as well as making visits for Rush they treated patients at his home. They bled the ill in the house, and when there was not room they took patients outdoors in the yard. For want of enough bowls to receive the blood, they often allowed it to flow out on the ground where it putrified.

Rush's mother stayed with him. The doctor described the household as the life of a wilderness.

Then Johnny Stall fell ill, just after his master's

recovery. Next, Fisher. Johnny Alston was in bed at his boardinghouse. Rush's home became a hospital. Even his sister began to fail. Marcus, the Negro, put up powders, induced blisters, and gave clysters—as well as any apothecary in town, Rush said. Two Negro nurses were brought in to care for the apprentices. In the household crisis, eleven-year-old Peter not only took over chores but one evening visited two patients for Rush.

That was the day when thirty-three persons were buried in potter's field alone before three o'clock in the afternoon. "In the midst of death I am in life," the doctor, paraphrasing, wrote Julia. "But O! by how tender a thread do I now hold it. I feel as if I were in a storm at sea in an open boat without helm or compass. My only hope and refuge Thou knowest, O God, is in Thee!"

At half-past twelve in the afternoon of September 23 Johnny Stall died. His death shocked Rush. He had been especially fond of his nineteen-year-old pupil. John Alston in his boardinghouse was next to go. Rush described how he had seen him "three times in a disease which required three and thirty visits. He refused to be bled for nearly a whole day because I was unable to visit him, and life and death often turn upon the application of a remedy at an hour or a moment in this ferocious disease."

Rush discovered an odd phenomenon connected with the fever. Those stricken with it had a tendency to deny that they had it, not only to themselves but to their doctors. He described this symptom: "I did not for many weeks meet with a dozen patients who acknowledged that they had any other indisposition than a common cold, or a slight remitting or intermittent fever. I was particularly struck with this self-deception in many persons who had nursed relations that died with the yellow fever, or who had been exposed to its contagion in families, or neighborhoods, where it had prevailed for days and even weeks with great mortality."

Part of this tendency toward self-deception Rush blamed on Kuhn's publications which advised the public that much of the epidemic was not yellow fever at all. Yet that was not all the explanation, he realized. Johnny Stall, from the beginning of his illness, objected to taking the medicine and deceived all around him in his accounts of how it worked. This was in spite of all his own experience with ill patients and his familiarity with Rush's emphasis on early treatment.

Toward the end of September, Rush's sister became dangerously ill. She had the disease for three days before she would take a dose of medicine, or let herself be bled. Her refusal to acknowledge the danger of the illness only confirmed Rush's observation of what seemed to be one of its most characteristic symptoms.

The day on which Rebecca gave in and retired to her bed was a gloomy one for Rush. John Coxe, his last effective apprentice, was seized with fever and went home to his grandfather.

Dr. Redman himself had been afflicted that very day. Rush attended him, finding his old preceptor in great danger. Then Rush's mother fell ill and went to bed. Peter was the only person in the household strong enough to help his master. "At eight o'clock in the evening," Rush wrote in his account of the fever, "I finished the business of the day. A solemn stillness at that time pervaded the streets. In vain did I strive to forget my melancholy situation by answering letters, and by putting up medicines to be distributed next day among my patients. My faithful black man—Marcus—crept to my door and at my request sat down by the fire, but he added by his silence and dullness to the gloom which suddenly overpowered every faculty of my mind."

At two o'clock in the afternoon of October 1 Rush's sister Rebecca died. It was the cruelest blow yet sustained. The funeral was that night. The three persons following the hearse to the grave were Marcus, Peter, and Billy Gray from the African Church.

Half an hour after his sister's death, Dr. Rush was out again on his rounds. As he wrote Julia, "The King's business requires fidelity as well as haste."

At one o'clock in the morning of October 10 Rush was awakened by a violent attack of illness. Every symptom of the fever gripped him. He had seldom felt more pain. In the darkness of his room he thought of his wife and children, all so dear to him. He would not see them again. He well knew that recovery in his weak and exhausted state was hardly probable.

He waited in the dark until two o'clock, then called Marcus and also Fisher, who was asleep in the next room. Fisher's expression confirmed to Rush how sick he was. His apprentice bled him at once, easing the pain, and gave the doctor a dose and a half of the purge medicine. Rush threw it up. A second dose had the same result. But by morning the purge "operated downwards," as Rush described it, and relieved him so much he was able to sit up. The fever returned in the afternoon with accompanying sleepiness which he considered dangerous. Once again Fisher bled him. He felt better after that, but very weak. He had fits of fainting at night, which Marcus, sleeping in the room with him, relieved by giving him something to eat.

Benjamin Rush did not die of the yellow fever. He came as close to death as a man could through days of delirium, for his case proved more stubborn and severe than cases of most victims. But he recovered slowly, and through his convalescence still directed the work of his two remaining apprentices, Coxe and Fisher, for as long as the raging epidemic continued. A few other physicians, mostly young men who had been Rush's pupils at the University, helped carry on with his patients, using his purging and bloodletting methods. Despite his illness, Rush's influence went on.

## 11   The New Black Suit

THROUGHOUT the disaster the differences of opinion between Rush and the majority of Philadelphia's physicians remained a malignant and fantastic thing. The methods of extreme purging and bloodletting versus mild tonics, bark, and cold water baths could not have been more opposite. The dispute fought out in the public press left Philadelphians confused and angry.

Right or wrong according to 1793's standards, Benjamin Rush had been the only physician to advance new ideas and strategy for combating the frightful epidemic. Others relied on former methods. Rush was the revolutionist. He had always been a revolutionist. Like all good revolutionists, he was absolutely convinced he was right.

He testified on his own behalf, a fair procedure considering the criticism against him. Case after case he cited in his letters to his wife:

—"Mr. Meredith is well after three bleedings. Thinking people submit to my method of treating the disorder, but many, very many, follow that which was *dictated* by Dr. Shippen's learned and sagacious friend, Dr. Kuhn. A son of Samuel Morris in Second Street has died under it. Two other of his sons have recovered under my care by bleeding and purging."

—"Another lady . . . fell upon my neck and wept aloud for several minutes before she would let me enter her husband's room. They were patients of Kuhn's. They proposed a consultation, but I objected to it. I said I had a confidence in my remedies and that I must attend him alone or not at all. They consented to my proposal, and after three bleedings he recovered."

—"Mrs. Hutchinson [the doctor's widow] and child are both living. She recovered under my care, deserted by all her husband's political and medical friends."

—"Dr. Redman is better. He has been cured by the new remedy."

—"William Hall's only son has escaped by *six* and Master John Adams at Mr. Kepland's by *seven* bleedings. . . . Four of our neighbor Cresson's family owe their lives under God to the free use of the new remedies. . . . In short, to tell you of all the people who have been bled and purged out of the grave in our city would require a book nearly as large as the Philadelphia Directory."

—"I am again employed in Mr. Hammond's family. After curing four of the servants, a French physician was sent for a few weeks afterwards to his steward and to one of his maids. They both died. Mr. Fisher is now attending his groom. It is possible that Mr. Hammond was persuaded that my four cures in his family were only of the fall fever because I did not put the yellow color of the disorder in their faces. I put it in a more suitable place by means of the strong but safe mercurial purges."

—"At three o'clock this afternoon I received a visit from Richard Allen and Absalom Jones [Negroes]. They informed me that after most of the physicians were confined, they procured the printed directions for curing the fever, went among the poor who were sick, gave them the mercurial purges, bled them freely, and by those means saved the lives of between two and three hundred persons. This information gave me great pleasure, as it showed the safety of the medicines I had recommended."

86

—"Since the 10th of September," Rush wrote to a New York physician, "I have found bleeding, in addition to the mercurial purges, to be necessary in nineteen cases out of twenty. The pulse, the appearance of the blood, the spontaneous hemorrhages, and the weather (exclusive of the stimulus of the contagion) all indicated the use of the lancet. At first I found the loss of ten or twelve ounces of blood sufficient to subdue the pulse, but I have been obliged, gradually, as the season advanced, to increase the quantity to sixty, seventy, and even eighty ounces, and in most cases with the happiest effects. I have observed the most speedy convalescence where the bleeding has been most profuse, and as a proof that it has not been carried to excess I have observed in no instance the least inconvenience to succeed it. . . . I bleed not only in the exacerbations of the fever but likewise in its remissions and intermissions where I find a low, slow, but corded pulse. I have recovered two patients in whom it beat less than fifty strokes a minute."

In final emphasis Rush noted at the close of the epidemic the fact that of all the sick sent to Bush Hill, the hospital for the poor, two fifths died. "Ben Duffield and a Frenchman were the physicians. The new remedies were never used." Another contemporary account of the epidemic reports that of about a thousand persons admitted to Bush Hill, nearly five hundred died.

Rush summed up his record: "Under the most unfavorable circumstances of attendance from my own sickness, the sickness of my pupils, et cetera, I seldom lost more than one in twenty of all who passed through my hands."

In the yellow fever of 1793 more than four thousand persons died in Philadelphia, some 10 per cent of the total normal population of the city even including those thousands who had fled at the beginning. As late as 1813 a Pennsylvania doctor speaking of Rush declared: "It is probable that not less than six thousand of the inhabitants of Philadelphia were saved from death by purging and bleeding during the autumn of 1793."

The yellow fever was over, normal life resumed in Philadelphia, politics again took over interest. Rush had his house washed down and painted, gave the old suit he had worn throughout the epidemic to Marcus, and bought himself a new black suit. At last Julia could bring the family home. Because he might still have contagion Rush insisted on sleeping in a room adjoining hers—with the door between open. The grim days were becoming memories.

President Washington returned to town from Mount Vernon for the fall opening of Congress. Dr. Shippen, who was now the presidential family doctor, came back to Philadelphia, too.

Rush had kept careful notes all through the epidemic, following the custom usual with him of writing things down. He planned from the start to publish a book on the subject of the fever. He went so far as to delegate the task to another doctor to finish in the event of his own death. The physician so trusted was James Mease, a graduate the year before from the University of Pennsylvania and a firm supporter of Rush's theories.

The *Account of the Yellow Fever* was published within a few months after the epidemic. It presented a clearly-stated, logically developed exposition of Rush's revolutionary methods, including arguments to prove they were not revolutionary at all but had in fact their foundations on past experiences of many well-known men. This was his thoughtful contribution not alone to Philadelphia but to a whole world to which yellow fever was a dreaded terror.

The book was read far and wide, in America and Europe. German and Spanish translations were published abroad. Wherever it was read, controversy followed it.

Rush demanded acceptance of his theories. He found that no one man could easily turn tradition. When he failed in his demands, his bitterness went to extremes. Rejection of his ideas became to him an intensely personal insult.

Julia was aware of his mood. She cautioned him. She could see he was going unreasonably far in condemnation of fellow doctors. Rush remembered Miles Mervin, the schoolmaster, the children, the old people, Johnny Stall, his own sister. They were dead. But he promised Julia he would listen to her advice. "Indeed," he said, "I never intended to begin a controversy with them."

Nevertheless, he angrily resigned his place in the College of Physicians. He never became one of that group again.

*Porcupine*

# 12

## A Restless Man

FEBRUARY—Monday, the 3rd, 1794—this day William Cobbett moved his family to Philadelphia.

The nation's capital offered more opportunities for an English tutor, he believed, than Wilmington, Delaware. So he hired a cart to transport their possessions, and took his wife Nancy, eight months pregnant, and the baby Toney in a coach to the city. A friend had found for them a house to rent on Callowhill Street, near the Northern Liberties above the town's center.

Bundled in his greatcoat, with his broad-brimmed hat on his head, Cobbett sat brooding for most of the thirty-mile trip up the shore of the Delaware River. If at first he seemed a portly man, the appearance was deceptive. He was built big, and he was strong. Even sitting in the coach seat, his broad shoulders were squared with the discipline of a soldier. His heavy features softened each time one-year-old Toney turned to him with a stream of half-formed prattle, until the child finally fell asleep on his mother's lap.

Cobbett smiled at his wife, and she moved her lips into a soundless "Shh." Gently she made the sleeping Toney more comfortable, at the same time keeping him from pressing too closely on her extended stomach. The jolting of the coach was painful in her condition, and the new life within her did not help with its responsive motions. Cobbett realized, and touched her hand by way of assurance.

Toney slept. William Cobbett glanced down at his son. The child had been seriously ill several months before. They had been afraid he might die. However hardheaded and practical Cobbett tried to be for himself, he was particularly sentimental and emotional about his family. His wife and child—and the new one coming—were close to his heart. Anything he believed worth while in relation to the rest of the world was justified by its meaning to his own, Nancy and Toney and the child to be.

Cobbett was thirty-one in this year of 1794, and Nancy twenty. He was a restless man, but he always had been restless. Born the son of a farmer-innkeeper in Surrey, England, he had run away from home twice before he left his family permanently at the age of twenty.

The first of these escapades, when he was only eleven, provided an experience which indelibly influenced his later career. He stayed away from home all night, and although he had little education beyond what his father could teach him, he knew how to read. Somewhere he found and bought for threepence a little book called *Tale of a Tub*. He took it to the side of a haystack and read until it was too dark to read more. He slept, and by the first light of day continued reading.

He had never heard of Jonathan Swift at that age,

and much of the book he could not understand. Yet the power of Swift's satiric writing made such an impression on his mind that later he said it had produced in him "a sort of birth of intellect." He kept that copy for years, until one day for some reason it dropped overboard at sea.

William Cobbett had used a seven-year enlistment term in the British Army as a springboard to his own self-education. Besides his soldier's duties he studied grammar, writing, reading. His knapsack was his bookcase, a bit of board his table. He was sent abroad to Nova Scotia, then New Brunswick, and turned his learning into profit by writing regimental reports for his officers. The initiative on his part earned for him a promotion to sergeant major.

He met Nancy while he was a soldier in New Brunswick. She was the daughter of an artillery sergeant. The story of their courtship reveals the intentness of purpose of which Cobbett was capable. He was introduced to Ann Reid and sat in the room with her, in the company of other people, for an hour. Rather than listen to the conversation, he watched her. She was beautiful, he thought. On the spot he selected her for his wife. But Ann Reid was only thirteen and he just short of twenty-four.

Three days later he passed her house on a very early morning walk. Two other soldiers from the barracks were with him. It was winter, the cold was piercing, and the snow several feet deep. The hour was so early it was scarcely daylight. Yet he found Ann outside her house, standing in the snow, scrubbing clothes in a washtub.

"There!" Cobbett said proudly to his companions. "That is the girl for me!"

As far as he was concerned, he said, the matter was as settled as if written in the book of Fate. However, the artillery regiment was soon transferred back to England, and with it went Ann Reid and her father. Before she left, the pair reached an understanding. More than four years passed before he could follow from overseas, but she was waiting faithfully.

He trusted her so completely that, when she left New Brunswick, he had given her all his savings, one hundred and fifty guineas, with instructions she was free to use it if she needed it to live comfortably. Yet when he found her again in England, she was working as a domestic. She returned his money untouched.

Nancy, as he fondly came to call her, could not write or easily read. Yet Cobbett said of her, "One hair of her head is more dear to me than all the other women of the world."

They were married in England at just about the time Cobbett discreetly fled from the country. The episode making his quick absence necessary marked Cobbett's initiation into the methods of polemics. He had discovered during his military service that the higher command of the regiment was steeped in graft and corruption. Cobbett's sense of righteousness and zeal for justice to the rank-and-file soldiers aroused him to action. After his discharge he attempted to bring former officers to court-martial.

He discovered almost too late that graft reached into too high places. He escaped in time the crushing weight of an army plot to have him jailed for bringing false charges.

It seemed never to have occurred to young Cobbett that equal corruption reached beyond the army into the rest of His Majesty's government.

He took his Nancy on a honeymoon to France. In six months he acquired knowledge of the language. The Revolution and imminent Anglo-French war sent the couple hurriedly to America—a destination fulfilling a long-time plan of Cobbett's.

They settled first in Wilmington, Delaware, as the

96

best place in Cobbett's opinion for a stranger to get his bearings. For a year and a half he earned a living in that town by teaching English to French émigrés from the West Indies.

Cobbett came to America restlessly, looking for a bright land of opportunity and freedom. He had every intention of becoming a citizen. He was disillusioned with the country. He found the land full of rocks, houses wretched, roads impassable. The weather was detestable, either burning hot or freezing cold. He saw no autumn or spring in the English fashion to which he was accustomed. He believed America was unhealthy, with every month of the year having its particular malady—fevers, vomitings, and other illnesses. The yellow fever in Philadelphia the previous summer and autumn proved his belief.

He suspected the people to be worthy of the country. A sly, roguish gang, he called Americans. Natives born here were by nature idle, and lived by cheating. Only foreigners of his acquaintance, being industrious, maintained their integrity. Yet in spite of all this, it was possible, particularly for Englishmen, to make fortunes here. This country was good for making money. In every other respect it was miserable.

The first period of settling in America was formative. Cobbett did well financially with his teaching, and he had written a book on English grammar for French students which he expected to have published in Philadelphia. Yet he sought after something else—he did not know what. He kept trying to push himself through a cloud of uncertainty in his mind.

Cobbett was driven by an urge to make the most of his life, to create of himself an individual of value. During his time in the British Army he had gone far. He described how he had given to the private soldiers of his regiment the perfect example of sobriety, economy, and of patient endurance of hardships. He knew that he could say to anyone that the lives of few men were marked with stronger proof of merit and character.

He did not plan to rest on his self-approbation. The man he had made of himself had power. Whatever he did, Cobbett was convinced he could reach the top of success. By going to Philadelphia, he expected to find better opportunities. If not, he could travel farther, perhaps to the West Indies.

Nancy had a faraway gaze in her eyes as she watched the countryside move past. The stagecoach was drawing near to Philadelphia. He wondered whether she thought, as he did, of what lay ahead for them. He had a planned self-confidence. Nancy, he suspected, was more than a little frightened.

## 13 The Birth of Peter Porcupine

PHILADELPHIA in the winter of 1794 seemed to have forgotten the summer's yellow fever. Cobbett on his arrival found the city in a pitch of fever about other things. An Englishman, he discovered that the anti-British feeling ran near to frenzy.

Of the rage and violence of the time, he said, speaking of this city new to him, no man not upon the spot could form any idea.

Yet it was not difficult to understand. From Philadelphia, as a major port of the country, ships sailed daily to United States and foreign places. And as fast, news kept coming in of vessels seized by British warships, cargoes confiscated, crews captured under London's Orders in Council. That the English actions were part of the strategy to

98

prevent neutral supplies from reaching the French was not justification to Americans. The British seizures were acts of piracy. Demands for war rose high.

Such feelings fanned into fire the anti-British, pro-French coals of the Democratic-Republicans. The Federalists might speak of French atheism, of French bloodshed at the guillotine. These undeniable sins of the French were of minor importance to foes of the British. The two political parties split further asunder on the English and French issues.

President Washington had proclaimed neutrality for the country. Citizen Genêt, minister from France in Philadelphia the previous year, violated ethics and his own promises by sending out privateers from American ports against the British. Congress, preserving neutrality, demanded his recall. The new minister from France arrived with orders for Genêt's arrest, but Washington granted him asylum. Genêt became a citizen and married the daughter of Governor Clinton of New York.

Such attitude of neutrality by the government did not reach down into the Philadelphia public. Mobs ran through the streets decrying everything British. The King was burned in effigy. Public opinion demanded that British reminders from colonial days be swept out: all customs and references to English ways, English procedures in courts, even the language. A serious proposal was considered that the English language be amended to an Americanized version.

Seeing the danger, and understanding that the problems between the United States and Great Britain must be settled short of war, in this year President Washington sent John Jay to England to negotiate a treaty of reconciliation.

Cobbett held his peace, and busied himself with his teaching. So far, he cared nothing about politics. He let hot feelings, partisan spirits, and boiling international in-

99

trigues swirl around him. As an Englishman, he kept his head down and tended to his own business.

Yet the more he heard against England, the stronger and more stubborn became his loyalty. By contrast to America, to him an increasingly detestable place, England became idyllic. He seemed to have forgotten that he was out of touch with the political unrest of that country, too. Distance softened reality. Cobbett became defensively patriotic and did not appear to realize that the untarnished glory of British monarchy lay mostly in his own mind.

Then, suddenly, tragedy struck the family, twice in quick succession, and William Cobbett had no heart for anything at all.

In the middle of March his Nancy went into labor. After long and dreadful suffering she gave birth to a baby boy. It was dead. This shock was scarcely over before Toney became ill. Frantically Cobbett called in two physicians. A Dr. Ball was one, the other, Dr. William Budd, who remained Cobbett's family physician throughout his Philadelphia stay except for a brief interlude later recorded in the trial proceedings.

After a long time of terrible worry, little Toney died.

Cobbett and his wife were beside themselves with grief. All that he had ever felt before seemed to be nothing, Cobbett cried, nothing compared to this. They had adored their son, the baby just beginning to talk. Moody sorrow oppressed him, softened only by his own distress for the utterly heartbroken state of his poor Nancy.

One of Cobbett's students was a Frenchman for whom he cared little. This man had political leanings which Cobbett resented—too republican. Though he was a refugee himself from the Revolution, the Frenchman was lukewarm about the whole system of monarchy. To Cobbett, such an attitude on the student's part was contemptible, and practically traitorous to his former sovereign. He compared the student to what Englishmen at home called slightingly "a coffeehouse politician."

It happened that on a day in June the French pupil brought along a newspaper as his homework assignment. Cobbett often had students read current papers and periodicals. The paper contained an article about Dr. Joseph Priestley, the famous English scientist and philosopher. That article was the one the Frenchman chose to read to his tutor, chuckling gleefully the while.

Priestley, clergyman and physicist, was one of the best-known Englishmen of his time, the discoverer of oxygen, formerly intimate friend of Benjamin Franklin. He was one of the English liberals carrying on the Wilkes' campaign for greater democracy in Britain. Outspoken in criticism of the monarchy and in sympathy with the French Revolution, he had brought upon himself the anger of the King and government. He migrated to America, a land more receptive to his philosophy of the individual's rights to freedom.

On his arrival in New York Priestley became an object of considerable attention. During welcoming ceremonies he made remarks derogatory to the autocracy of Britain's government, and urged the necessity of liberal reform in England. Some of these remarks were published in Philadelphia papers. The article read aloud by Cobbett's student came from one of these publications.

The student agreed with Priestley. He needled Cobbett by adding his own scornful comments.

In Cobbett's view, it was one thing for a Frenchman or American to express disapprobation of the English king. But for an Englishman to do so was another matter entirely. Cobbett's round face flushed angrily as he heard his pupil read Priestley's words. Cobbett thought Priestley uttered not criticisms, but invectives. Priestley, he cried, was no reformer but a traitor.

101

Cobbett was touchy anyway. Toney's death still hung over him. He did not like this French student. He had writhed in silence under the denunciation he had been hearing against his beloved homeland. The combination of these things created an explosive force inside the English tutor. The newspaper article read by the student that day provided a spark.

He declared his resentment to the student. The Frenchman thought the whole thing was funny. Cobbett exploded, and so did the Frenchman. The English lesson was quickly forgotten. Even considering the French nature of his student, Cobbett found the man had an uncommonly violent temper. So had Cobbett. Their argument grew hot. Yet it might have ended as merely another political disagreement except for one thing. During the course of the conversation Cobbett stated that he would write a pamphlet, as an Englishman, in defense of his own country. The Frenchman took it up as a challenge. He pledged himself to write an answering pamphlet.

The student never followed through. Cobbett, however, began at once. He had suffered far too long the abuses poured on England. Denunciation of Britain had been too long left unchallenged. Here, he thought, was one Englishman who did not fear to stand up for his country and king, cost what it might in this unfriendly land.

In a blaze of patriotic fervor Cobbett wrote the pamphlet, some forty-seven pages long. He lashed at Priestley as a hypocrite. The doctor had criticized English mobs which demonstrated against him, Cobbett declared, but at the same time he sympathized with the revolutionary mobs of France. The doctor's ideas produced the very violence of which he complained, Cobbett said. Priestley was undermining established government.

In boiling anger, Cobbett found composing the pamphlet to be particularly satisfying. A grin of glee crossed his face as he described Priestley's writing ability: "As to his talents as a writer, we have only to open our eyes to be convinced that they are far below mediocrity. His style is uncouth and superlatively diffuse. Every sentence is a string of parentheses, in finding the end of which the reader is lucky if he does not lose the proposition they were meant to illustrate. In short, the whole of his phraseology is extremely disgusting."

He paused thoughtfully as he wrote. The words and sentences seemed to flow naturally from his mind. There must have been echoes of Jonathan Swift guiding him. He read his manuscript again, nodded with grim enjoyment. He would show Dr. Joseph Priestley what it meant to attack his own sovereign king.

He found a publisher for the completed pamphlet. Thomas Bradford in Philadelphia agreed to print and sell it, but the subject was so controversial that he insisted it be done anonymously, not even the publisher himself daring to put his imprint on it. The title was *Observations on the Emigration of Dr. Joseph Priestley*.

The whole matter was an experiment, rather something to relieve his own angry feelings than a premeditated effort on Cobbett's part. The results were startling.

The small book became a sensation, a best seller. It ran through a number of editions. It was republished in England. The reaction on both sides of the Atlantic was immense.

For once, someone challenged the prevailing tide of democracy. Federalists in America and monarchists in England were alike delighted. The pamphlet was a treatise for law and order, opposed to radical policies of Priestley and his associates.

But the liberals—Radicals in England and Democratic-Republicans in America—were outraged. Their esteemed Dr. Priestley was held up to contempt. Countercharges flew. Publications of rebuttal appeared. Who was the author? liberals demanded. In spite of the pamphlet's anonymity, Cobbett had aroused a real storm.

No one suspected the unknown tutor of Philadelphia.

At this point William Cobbett had much to think about. He had been searching for the purpose of his life. The pamphlet proved that, inexperienced though he was, he had a natural skill in writing satire. Somehow he had achieved in this, his first work of its kind, a remarkable technique. His ability, he thought, must be natural to him. His delight as an eleven-year-old boy in reading *The Tale of a Tub* beside a haystack was at long last explained.

Seeing the storm stirred up by his pamphlet, Cobbett squared his shoulders and the glint of battle came into his eyes. His acute perception told him that he had by accident stumbled across the challenge for which he had moulded himself. His blood caught fire. He reached again for his pen.

Thus, he declared, it was that he became a writer on politics.

*Observations on the Emigration of Dr. Joseph Priestley* was published in August, 1794. That summer William Cobbett took his wife out to the country. Both of them needed a change from the house on Callowhill Street where they had known the depths of tragedy. So they missed the mild epidemic of yellow fever in Philadelphia in the late summer of that year.

The quiet of the country helped Cobbett make his plans. Could he repeat the success of his first book, he wondered. The field of politics, he discovered, embraced the broadest opportunities. Why—here was Cobbett's sharp perception at work—why shouldn't he become in America the defender of England, but this time without limiting his targets to disloyal Englishmen?

104

Anti-monarchy was the root of all political unrest. Anti-monarchy led to the revolutions in America and in France. So-called republicans, the supporters of revolt against kings, stirred up all the trouble. Cobbett decided he must strike out at republicans, all republicans, everywhere, whether they be breeds of traitorous English, insolent Americans, or blood-soaked Frenchmen.

At this time Cobbett had not one trace within himself of republican principles. He abhorred democratic ideas. He was thoroughly loyal to his king. English at heart, Tory to the core, he was an ideal monarchist.

His plan expanded. His chief weapon of attack would be laughter. With sarcasm and ridicule he would hold up his foes to public eyes as ludicrous. With laughter he would swamp the enemies of English monarchy so they would hide their faces away.

Cobbett wrote a new pamphlet, called *A Bone to Gnaw for the Democrats*. He aimed at democratic societies in Philadelphia, at supporters of republican causes, and at newspapers sympathetic to the French. One of them was the *Aurora,* published by Franklin Bache, grandson of Benjamin Franklin. The *Aurora* was the chief mouthpiece of the Democratic-Republican party and a vigorous foe of Federalism. The newspaper was a formidable opponent for the English tutor to take on at the start of a writing career.

The weapon worked. The second pamphlet sold as well as the first. He followed it with a third, entitled *A Kick for a Bite*. With savage mockery he attacked personalities and principles. The books caused indignant roars, but their devastating effects could not be ignored. Leaders of both Federalist and the Democratic-Republican parties began to consider the unknown writer a serious factor in politics.

A current magazine review said of the books that the

105

author had two purposes, "To rescue the British character from the general obloquy attached to it; the other to depress, in the popular opinion, the name as well as the principles of the democrats." His method, the review stated, was the use of "simple laughter—his magical pen throws every object into a ludicrous light, and determined to make the most of the ridiculous, he laughs almost without cessation from the beginning of his book to the end of it."

Cobbett still lacked something. He could not reveal himself by using his own name for his writing. To do that would give away the mystery which helped to sell the books. Writing anonymously provided no personality identification in the public mind. He needed a pseudonym.

He signed his third book "Peter Porcupine." What better name, he thought, to describe what he planned to do?

## 14 "A Very Extraordinary Creature"

IN THE next two years William Cobbett went far.

His burly figure moving deliberately around the streets became a familiar sight to Philadelphians. Usually wearing a red waistcoat under his coat and a broad-brimmed hat on his head, he was unmistakable. His writing and the brilliant sarcasm of his barbed words were unmistakable, too.

As a writer, Cobbett was cold, calculating, and sardonic. He used his special kind of mind to sort out truths and half-truths, turning them into sharp-edged quips. He became a master at making the objects of his scorn squirm in the ridicule he turned on them.

Cobbett had a single, clear-cut purpose for his writing. He meant to change public opinion in the United States away from republican feelings, French sympathies, and

106

democratic principles. He was determined to restore instead American respect to Britain and the King.

In time the whole United States came remarkably close to accepting the ideas which William Cobbett poured out in his publications from Philadelphia.

Peter Porcupine became a vocal supporter of Alexander Hamilton's policies. The Federalists had quickly discovered in him their loudest and most potent mouthpiece. He began to be read by more people than any other writer of his time. He had more influence, in proportion to the population, than any other writer of his kind then, or probably since. He published nine issues of a somewhat erratic monthly periodical, and he started his own daily newspaper which he called *Porcupine's Gazette*. He wrote a stream of pamphlets, after the custom of those days. By his own claims, he scored a number of victories.

One of those he claimed was the Jay Treaty with England. The treaty which John Jay, at Washington's orders, drew up in draft form with the British Government in 1794 settled the long-outstanding disputes left over from the War of Independence and resolved a compatible relationship with Britain for the future. The Democratic-Republicans and the majority of the American people were opposed to any such treaty with their old enemy. Its ratification would cause a rift with France, they cried. Demonstrations against the Jay Treaty flared up in 1795 all over the country, and even President Washington, himself in favor of the treaty, hesitated to sign it.

Into this tangle William Cobbett threw himself with heart and soul. He turned out pamphlets favoring the treaty, scored those who opposed it. By words and pen he fought for months for the treaty's ratification, castigating personalities of congressmen who would not vote for it.

After months of heated discussion Congress finally

did approve the treaty by a narrow margin in April, 1796. Cobbett took the credit. He never was a reticent man. He said that he became in America, beginning in 1794, a most industrious, zealous, and able defender of England's rights. According to everyone, he declared, the Jay Treaty would never have been ratified by the Senate if it had not been for the influence of his publications. It was *his* treaty, he said with unabashed candor, rather than the treaty of Mr. Jay and the English minister.

He flaunted his English patriotism in Philadelphia's face. He rented a house on Second Street, opposite Christ Church and not far from where Benjamin Franklin once lived, and opened a bookshop and printing business there. In that way he could publish all his own works. Taking the house meant a public revelation that Peter Porcupine was in reality William Cobbett, an Englishman. It could have been a fatal admission.

Peter Porcupine had dared write things about England and George III that no one else had said since before the Revolution. He was detested by liberal republicans, hated vengefully by men he had attacked. Cobbett knew there were thousands in Philadelphia who would have been glad to see him murdered by a mob. And only a very few, he believed, would have stirred an inch to save him.

It was typical of Cobbett to defy the danger. When he opened his bookshop, he thought he had to go all the way in his defiance. By hesitation he would be lost. So, on the Sunday before the new store opened, he worked all day on a window display. He filled his windows with pictures of kings, queens, princes, and nobles, including all the English ministry, bishops, judges, admirals. Every item that could possibly enrage Great Britain's enemies he used. Among them was a picture of "Lord Howe's Decisive Victory over the French." Not for years until Cobbett had

108

anyone dared put into a window a portrait of George III himself.

Nancy Cobbett was quiet, timid. They had a new baby now. She was anxious. People would break into the house, destroy everything, kill or injure all three of them. Cobbett stayed firm. On Monday morning he took down the shutters from his windows.

The reaction was fast enough. People passing stopped, gaped. Word spread through the city. The street filled. Angry muttering grew into threats. Cobbett stood his ground, and nothing happened. His challenge, by its very bravado, overwhelmed the mob.

So William Cobbett introduced his name to Philadelphians.

In his writing Cobbett used the sneering word, the sentence of twisting innuendo. His method was a continuous assault against political personalities, trying to bring them down by repeated derision. Few on the opposite side of the political fence were exempt.

Peter Porcupine prophesied of "Citizen" Madison: "As a politician he is no more; he is absolutely deceased, cold, stiff, and buried in oblivion forever more." He referred to Lafayette as a fancy fellow who had been so much improved by living in a dungeon that it was a pity, he thought, he had not remained there forever. He told Noah Webster, ardent supporter of democracy, that he would have "the heart-killing mortification to see another king on the throne of France, which he will see though he should ride through Connecticut to pick up a collection of John Knox's thundering curses to hurl on the heads of the royalists!" The memory of Benjamin Franklin, patriarch of American liberty, was gall to Cobbett. He implied that Franklin, "Old Lightning Rod," had been involved with graft in connection with an arms shipment from France.

109

He referred sarcastically to rumors of Franklin's fathering illegitimate children: "As a moralist the doctor's *example* is certainly a useful one, more especially in a country like this that is thinly inhabited. 'Increase and multiply' is an injunction that this great man had continually in his mind and such was his zeal in the fulfillment of it, that he paid very little attention to time or place or person."

Porcupine addressed Thomas Jefferson in the following manner:

"No, Monsieur Thomas; the sun of Britain will shine; her philosophy will illuminate an admiring world, and her freedom (her *real* freedom) will continue to be 'the charter of the land,' when thy head will be rotting cheek by jowl with that of some toil-killed Negro slave. She will flourish in commerce, in art, and in arms, when thy *pivot-chair* shall be crumbled into dust; when thy French-spun theories, thy flimsy philosophy, thy shallow shifting politics, and thy envious vindictive predictions shall all be damned to eternal oblivion. . . ."

The newspaper war between Cobbett and Franklin Bache raged on to the public's delight. Cobbett outdid himself for the benefit of Hamilton's party. Bache's *Aurora* was the principal publication for the views of Jeffersonians. Each publisher attempted to tear the other to shreds.

Bache printed a letter alleged to have been signed by "Paul Hedgehog," asserting that Cobbett was in the pay of a British agent. Cobbett retorted in kind. They sparred in their respective columns until Cobbett wearied of the game and published this final reply: "Those who still believe the lies that have been vomited forth against me are either too stupid or too perverse to merit further attention. I will therefore never write another word in reply to anything that is published about myself. Bark

110

away, hell hounds, till you are suffocated in your own foam."

Besides Cobbett writing for the Federalists was a publisher named John Fenno, friend and protégé of Alexander Hamilton. Fenno produced a newspaper called *The United States Gazette.* He lacked the brilliance of Cobbett, but his writings were scarcely more dignified. Cobbett and Fenno together gave public expression to the policies of the Federalists.

Then in 1796 an exchange of public letters occurred which set William Cobbett far ahead of Fenno in political importance. The rumor reached Philadelphia of Thomas Paine's death in France. After his success in the American Revolution, Paine had returned as an American citizen to England. There he wrote his incendiary book *The Rights of Man,* was accused of trying to inspire a British revolution against the Crown, and indicted for treason. Before the trial he escaped to France, in time to take part in the French Revolution. Though English by birth and American by naturalization, Paine found himself elected to the revolutionary French Convention.

By intrigues of American, English, and French inspiration—a strange story in itself—Paine was put into prison by the revolutionists. The report arose that he had died there. Yet before his arrest Paine had published the first part of his anti-Christian philosophy, *Age of Reason,* a tract which alienated in disgust many of his former American and English friends. Absurd and impious Benjamin Rush called it, but he did admit that Thomas Paine had demoralized half the Christian world.

William Cobbett considered Paine the arch-devil of all revolutionary and republican ideas. He was not only a born Englishman who had treacherously taken part in the American war against his own king, but he had similarly promoted rebellion in England itself. Only to cap

111

his iniquity, Cobbett thought, he had shared in the bloody business in France.

On the rumor of Paine's death, Cobbett honored him with a published epitaph—in verse:

When the wight who here lies beneath the cold earth
First quitted the land that had given him birth
He commenc'd the apostle of Bloodshed and strife,
And practic'd the trade to the end of his life.
Sedition and nonsense and lies to dispense,
He took up the title of "Old Common Sense";
Taught poor honest men how rich rogues to keep under,
Excited to pillage and shared in the plunder;
But when there no longer was plunder to share,
His "common sense" led him to seek it elsewhere.
To his countrymen now he returned back again,
The wronger of rights and the *righter of men;*
He told them they still were a nation of slaves,
That their king was a fool, and his ministers knaves,
And the only sure way for the people to thrive
Was to leave neither one nor the other alive.
But Thomas who never knew when he should stop,
Went a little too far and was catch'd on the hop.
In short, 'twas determined that poor Tom should lose
His ears at a post, or his life in a noose.
"Old Common Sense" boggles, then skulks out of sight,
Then packs up his rags and decamps in the night.
His arrival at Paris occasions a fete,
And he finds in the den of assassins a seat.
Here he murders, and thieves, and makes laws for a season;
Is crammed in a dungeon and preaches up—"Reason":
Blasphemes the Almighty, lives in filth like a hog,
Is abandon'd in death, and interr'd like a dog.
Tom Paine for the devil is surely a match:
In hanging Old England he cheated Jack-Catch;
In France (the first time such a thing had been seen)
He cheated the watchful and sharp Guillotine;
And at last, to the sorrow of all the beholders,
He marched out of life with his head on his shoulders.

Cobbett had attacked Paine consistently. The influence of Peter Porcupine's pamphlets reached far out from Philadelphia. Paine in France, not dead at all and finally out of prison, saw Porcupine's writings. Paine also was hurt and angry at President George Washington for what he believed was the President's failure to use influence to get him out of jail sooner. Reading Porcupine's attacks, he was angrier still. One injustice was piled on top of another. Paine linked Washington and Cobbett as Federalists.

Thomas Paine wrote his long, violent *Letter to Washington,* censuring the President for just about everything under the sun including his past military record. Furthermore, he wrote, "Had I wanted a commentary of his [Washington's] silence with respect to my imprisonment in France, some of his faction has furnished me with it. What I here allude to is a publication in a Philadelphia paper, copied afterward into a New York paper, both under the patronage of the Washington faction [meaning the Federalists], in which the writer, still supposing me in prison in France, wonders at my lengthy respite from the scaffold; and he marks his politics still further by saying: 'It appears, moreover, that the people of England did not relish his [Thomas Paine's] opinion quite so well as he expected, and after one of his last pieces, as destructive to the peace and happiness of their country (meaning, I suppose, *The Rights of Man*), they threatened our knight-errant with such serious vengeance that, to avoid a trip to Botany Bay, he fled over to France as a less dangerous voyage.'

"I am not refuting or contradicting the falsehood of this letter," Paine went on, "for it is sufficiently notorious; neither am I censuring the writer: on the contrary, I thank him for the explanation he has incautiously given of the principle of the Washington faction. Insignificant, however, as the piece is, it was capable of having some small ill effects had it arrived in France during my imprisonment, and in the time of Robespierre; and I am not un-

113

charitable in supposing that this was one of the intentions of the writer"—meaning it could well have been the cause of getting Paine promptly guillotined.

Paine continued in a note, "I know not who the writer of the piece is . . . he writes under the signature of Peter Skunk, or Peter Porcupine, or some such signature."

Franklin Bache published Paine's *Letter to Washington* in the *Aurora,* and it was republished for the whole American and European public as well. The letter coincided with the political campaign of 1796 and immediately became an important part of it. Even though Washington would not be a candidate for a third term, he was by now quite firmly a part of Hamilton's Federalist party. To discredit Washington would also undermine the Federalists, and Paine's *Letter* did just that. Whatever Paine's reputation morally, he could write convincingly for the public. Paine had been at Washington's right hand through most of the War of Independence. Few people could have been in a more strategic position to criticize the general.

Cobbett jumped to action in the Federalist emergency. With the election not long off, he fired back at Paine. Referring to the *Letter,* he said, "I have no room here to say anything as to the contents of this superlatively insolent and infamous performance; but it is clear that the old ruffian [Paine] has been ordered to write it by the 'French convention.'" He referred to "the sweepings of Tom's brain," and said, "nor have I the least doubt but they [the French] are now enjoying the hope that General Washington's head is kicking about the streets of Philadelphia."

Cobbett took the opportunity to do his own electioneering. Referring to Thomas Jefferson, leading candidate for the Democratic-Republican party, Peter Porcupine stormed savagely:

". . . a man as fit to be president as I am to be an

114

archbishop! A man who is a deist by profession, a philosopher by trade, and a Frenchman in politics and morality; a man who has written a passport for Tom Paine's *Rights of Man,* and would if necessary write another for his infamous *Letter to General Washington;* a man, in short, who is at the head of the prostituted party by whose intrigue he has been brought forward and is supported. If this man is elected president, the country is sold to the French; and, as plantations are generally sold with livestock on them, I shall remove my carcass; for I'm resolved never to become their property. I do not wish my family vault to be in the guts of cannibals."

Cobbett wrote his own *Letter to Paine.* It was a carefully worded refutation of Paine's charges against Washington. Point by point, with argument and ridicule and by quoting Paine's own previous praises of Washington, Cobbett dissected Paine's criticism. He told Paine scathingly: "Your brutal attempt to blacken his [Washington's] character was all that was wanted to crown his honor and your infamy. The vile democrats, nay even Franklin Bache with whom you boast in being in close correspondence, can say not a word in its defense."

The Federalists acclaimed this important defense of Washington. It was especially effective considering that support to the former commander in chief of the armies which defeated the British had come from Cobbett, an avowed and extreme English monarchist. Much of the sting was drawn from Paine's attack, and the supporters of Hamilton had gained an invaluable weapon for the coming presidential battle.

Peter Porcupine, immensely popular, had lifted himself to the rank of highest influence in American politics. Referring to his *Letter to Paine,* George Washington himself wrote to a friend, "Inclosed also you will receive a production of *Peter Porcupine,* alias William Cobbett.

115

Making allowances for the asperity of an Englishman, for some of his strong and coarse expressions and a want of official information of many facts, it is not a bad thing."

And even Abigail Adams said of him, "Peter says many good things . . . that man is a very extraordinary creature . . . his shafts are always tipt with wit."

In the following election the electoral vote for the presidency gave John Adams, Federalist, a majority of three votes over Thomas Jefferson, Democratic-Republican. At that time the runner-up for the presidency became vice-president. One can only conjecture how much influence William Cobbett had on the Federalist victory. At the least, if Cobbett was the tail, the dog was beginning to wag.

# Freedom of the Press

# 15

## The Rittenhouse Eulogium

BENJAMIN RUSH had firmly resolved to withdraw from public affairs and politics. He did not even vote in the presidential election of 1796. He thought highly of all the major candidates—John Adams and Thomas Pinckney, Federalists, and Jefferson and Aaron Burr, Democratic-Republicans. Both Adams and Jefferson were close friends of his, and the doctor kept aloof. He had been embroiled in enough controversies. He wanted no more than to take care of his medical career.

His practice was already in a half-demoralized state, as it had been since the yellow-fever epidemic in 1793. The fever had come again in 1795 and 1796 but not in epidemic proportions. Rush had the satisfaction of seeing many of his opponents among the physicians come over to his debilitating treatment. They used bleeding and purging not only for the yellow fever but for other diseases. Dr. Kuhn, Rush found, was bleeding patients by the quart. He heard of an instance where Dr. Currie and Dr. Wistar took from a man suffering with pleurisy a hundred and three ounces of blood.

But the hostility to Rush remained alive. The gap between the profession resolved itself into a question of terminology. What Rush called yellow fever, others said was jaundice. Treatments of diseases varied widely. And the argument over the origin of yellow fever raged unabated.

The people of Philadelphia had to make a difficult decision: whether to place their faith on Rush and the doctors of his school of practice, or on the opposite faction of conservative, cautious doctors under the influence of Shippen and Kuhn. In Rush's group, besides James Mease, his friend and former student, were two newcomers, Dr. William Dewees lately moved to Philadelphia, and Philip Syng Physick, destined to become one of America's leading surgeons. Among the others against Rush were Benjamin Duffield, and especially his one-time friend William Currie, who seemed to be waiting vindictively for a chance to destroy Rush's reputation.

University students, too, had to decide which faction to follow. Rush felt deeply the opposition's efforts to keep students out of his classes. Duffield condemned Rush in most of his lectures. Shippen did all he could to persuade students to attend Kuhn's courses instead of Rush's.

The doctor's reputation had suffered from the public dissensions of 1793. His practice stood still. The poor he always had, but new patients from prosperous families seldom came to him. Yet the series of books he was writing, on *Medical Inquiries and Observations,* brought him fame not only in the United States but also in Europe. He was specializing now in mental illness. He thought he had discovered that purging and bloodletting were especially effective in acute "mania" cases. He considered madness to be a state of fever. This phase of his practice did bring to
120

Dr. Rush increasing numbers of patients. He was becoming a recognized authority on mental illness.

At this point in Benjamin Rush's life a friend of his since early Revolutionary days died. He was a Philadelphian named David Rittenhouse, president of the American Philosophical Society. "Our great republican and philosophical friend," Rush called Rittenhouse in a letter to Thomas Jefferson. As a mark of respect, Dr. Rush offered to present a "eulogium" for him before the Philosophical Society.

Unfortunately for Rush's intentions to keep out of politics, his eulogium turned into a major treatise for Jeffersonian republicanism.

Delivery of the eulogium took place ten days after John Adams had been elected second president of the nation, with Thomas Jefferson of the opposite political party vice-president. They were to take office the following March.

David Rittenhouse is remembered in Philadelphia chiefly by the public square named in his honor. Here children roller skate and feed pigeons. The man himself was a clock and instrument maker by profession, as well as astronomer and meteorologist. He had played a part in the Revolution, been active in the early Pennsylvania government. Until shortly before his death he had been director of the United States Mint.

Nothing especially spectacular marked the career of David Rittenhouse. He was much respected, but compared to other Pennsylvanians of the time he was a lesser light.

Yet on December 17, 1796, a remarkable gathering took place. On this day the American Philosophical Society met in the First Presbyterian Church on Market Street to hear Dr. Rush deliver his paper for the purpose of perpetuating Rittenhouse's memory. Attending by invitation were President Washington, members of the Senate and House of Representatives, leaders of Pennsylvania, officials of foreign governments, and most influential persons of Philadelphia. A more highly elite group could not have gathered together in this capital city of the country.

Oratory had been a joy to Benjamin Rush since college days. He was emotional over the death of his esteemed friend. The doctor also believed that the nation he had helped to found was in a state of political apathy serious enough to sink its future. Standing before the President, the highest men of the government, and important citizens of his state and city, Dr. Rush relished the opportunity to speak his mind. He made the most of it.

The first three quarters of the oration kept to the subject, a eulogy of David Rittenhouse, his life, his scientific work, the qualities of his character. Rush spoke of his friend's great patriotism:

"His country, his beloved country, was the object of the strongest affections of his heart. For her he fought; for her he labored; and for her in the hours of difficulty and danger he wept—in every stage of the American Revolution. Patriots of 1776, you will acquit me of exaggeration here, for you feel in the recollection of what passed in your bosoms a witness of the truth of each of these assertions. The year of the Declaration of Independence which changed our royal governments into republics, produced no change in his political principles, for he had been educated a republican by his father. I can never forget the pleasure with which he avowed his early but secret attachment to an elective and representative form of government. Often have I heard him anticipate with delight the effects of our Revolution on sowing the seeds of a new order of things in other parts of the world. . . ."

After a time the doctor left Rittenhouse and went on for himself. Perhaps as a physician he made a mistake,
122

but he gave a speech which deserves to stand with the best of what Americans have expressed of their own particular way of life:

"It belongs to monarchies to limit the business of government to a privileged order of men, and it is from the remains of monarchical spirit in our country that we complain when clergymen, physicians, philosophers, and mechanics take an active part in civil affairs. The obligations of patriotism are as universal and binding as those of justice and benevolence. . . . Man was made for a republic, and a republic was made for man, otherwise Divine Power and goodness have been wasted. . . .

"Our philosopher [Rittenhouse] adopted this truth from the evidence of his feelings, in common with the rest of mankind, but it was strongly reinforced in his mind by numerous analogies of nature. How was it possible for him to contemplate light and air as the common and equal partners of every man, and not acknowledge that Heaven intended liberty to be distributed in the same manner among the whole human race! Or how could he behold the beauty and harmony of the universe, as the result of universal and mutual dependence, and not admit that Heaven intended rulers to be dependent upon those for whose benefit alone all governments should exist. To suppose to the contrary would be to deny unity and system in the plans of the great Creator of all things. I shall make no apology for these sentiments. May the time never come in which the praises of our republican government shall not be acceptable to the ears of an American audience! . . ."

This speech directly challenged the Federalists. Whether Rush intended to or not—and undoubtedly he did—it thrust at Alexander Hamilton's carefully constructed platform. Rush's clipped and defiant words were a clear call for the broad, liberal base of democracy in which he had always believed. George Washington, who

123

was less in favor of universal electoral suffrage than Thomas Jefferson, sat in his place and listened to his once-rebellious army doctor. Others present still thought the government of the English King and Parliament was a good and proper system. But Rush's liberal friends in the American Philosophical Society surely chuckled at his daring.

Among the listeners were those who would excuse the doctor by saying he was out of politics, this outburst was merely because he had been carried away. What he said was excusable because he was a physician.

But there were those who said to themselves: "This fool has already gone far enough. Now it is too much. We must get rid of him."

If John Adams had been in that audience, and probably he was, he would have forgiven Rush. He knew his old colleague too well to object to his being on the other side of the political fence. Adams himself was a liberal-minded conservative.

But if Alexander Hamilton was there, that would have been another story. Hamilton was not a forgiving man. He would have remembered, too, the episode of Rush's letter about Washington during the winter of Valley Forge.

Whether Hamilton was present or not matters little, for within a few days Rush's eulogium was printed and widely distributed. Few people missed reading it. Hamilton was surely not one of them.

The doctor had added troubles beyond measure for himself.

William Cobbett was not in the church on that day to hear Dr. Rush. The American Philosophical Society would never have invited him.

124

Cobbett read the eulogium, though. He obtained a printed copy, and read it carefully. His eyebrows rose, and he frowned. He did not relish Benjamin Rush's remarks. The doctor, however famous for his medical theories, was getting outside of his practice. The speech could hardly have been a more pointed attack on the monarchy of England.

Cobbett expected to print a new pamphlet for publication in January. It was to be filled with political items and miscellaneous matters. In that issue he would nullify the effect of the doctor's speech, and at the same time dispose of the memory of David Rittenhouse. The eulogium could be turned into an absurdity.

He sat down at his writing table, and took up his pen. The first phrases ran through his mind. He noted them down:

> . . . But what good did Rittenhouse do to mankind? Dr. Rush, indeed, says that he did a great deal, and particularly to his country. But with all due submission to the hyperbolical bombast of Dr. Rush and his eulogium on the politics of Dr. Rittenhouse, I never heard of any good thing to mankind, and particularly America, that he did except determining the boundaries of some of the states, "which he did with great precision," and which I could have done as well as he had I received the same pay for it . . .

Cobbett paused, pen held high. He glanced off into space, thinking. He wore his usual red waistcoat, with his jacket discarded while he worked. His hair was tousled.

He continued after a moment:

> The remorseless Dr. Rush shall bleed me till I am as white as this paper before I'll allow that this was doing good to mankind . . . a dry uninteresting narrative . . . so glaring a departure from truth that it will attract but little more respect for [Rittenhouse's] memory than the hogwash toasts of the factious Society of which he was president.

125

Another pause. Then:

> Dr. Rush is a very fine man, to be sure; and he writes in a fine doctor-like manner. Such is the zeal of Dr. Rush that he vows his friend was born a republican; though everyone knows that he was born under the royal government of Britain. But don't let us misconstrue the doctor; he means a mental republican. Born a mental republican! Upon my soul it is a wonder he had not traced his republicanism a little further back, and turned the eulogium on his deceased subject into a lecture on anatomy.

## 16   The Yellow Plague

THE year 1797 opened well enough for Benjamin Rush. His business, though not too good, seemed to be no worse. He looked forward to the graduation in August of his second son, Richard, from the College of New Jersey. Richard planned to enter law.

The article by Porcupine criticizing his Rittenhouse eulogium had appeared in January. The doctor ignored it. It meant only one more item in the long series of attacks he had borne all his life, and in itself the writing did no harm. He paid no attention even when Porcupine favored him with another notice in March advising that he was leaving to Dr. Rush under his will a copy of the aforesaid January issue of Cobbett's publication—"but upon the express condition that he does not in any wise or guise, either at the time of my death, or *six months after,* pretend to speak, write, or publish an eulogium on my calling or character."

But in July yellow fever struck Philadelphia once more. All the Philadelphia doctors had come by now to the use of calomel purges, and most of them were bleeding patients in greater or less degree. Rush had discovered that in addition to his other remedies the application of mer-

126

cury ointment to the body was invaluable. The purpose was to excite salivation or excess watering of the mouth. This was another method of "debilitation" to draw off body overstimulation.

The other doctors used mercury for salivation, too. One accelerated the action by putting socks filled with mercurial ointment on his patients' feet. Another physician accomplished the same result by injecting the ointment in a suitable vehicle into the bowels by clysters.

Yet the old argument over the name of the disease returned with increased asperity. None who recovered after plentiful bleeding and purging were admitted to have had the disease, Rush found with disgust, while most of those who died under different treatment were said to die of worms, falls, colds, and twenty other diseases.

The conflict over the fever's origin took a more bitter turn. Rush still claimed steadfastly that the disease originated locally. He insisted that to prevent it the city must clean up its swamps, the filth and refuse in the streets. The opposition disputed his argument. Not only doctors, but businessmen and politicians joined in the outcry declaring that the fever originated in the West Indies and came to Philadelphia by ship. Was Dr. Rush, they demanded, trying to destroy the good character of the city and drive away new inhabitants, business, and even Congress? Rush could ruin the city.

James Mease, now holding the position of port physician, sided with Rush. In a newspaper notice he pledged that no yellow fever had come in by sea. Dr. Currie, for the opposition, in another published notice implied that Mease really did not know what he was talking about.

William Cobbett's daily newspaper, *Porcupine's Gazette,* got into the argument almost unwillingly. Early in the epidemic Cobbett had written, "I do not intend to trouble the reader with many articles relating to this scourge of Philadelphia. I shall, perhaps, now and then insert an article of a medical nature; but I shall in general reject whatever is not either directly or indirectly connected with politics, or political character."

This definition of Cobbett's policy sounded sincere. However, a rash of letters from doctors of differing opinions came to his desk in every mail. Rush himself submitted one on the local origin subject. Cobbett printed most of the letters, and watched developments. Then he published an unsigned letter, addressed to Dr. Benjamin Rush: "As you persisted ever since the year 1793, annually, to generate a yellow fever for the chastisement of your native city, and never yet have satisfactorily accounted for your singular opinions on the subject, give me leave to propose to you the following queries, for further information."

The letter went on to ask why, when Philadelphia streets used to be unpaved and dead carcasses lay in every direction around the city, yellow fever was not generated in the town before 1793. Also, why did it not appear first in the more crowded sections where putrid substances and offensive smells were greater than other parts? Perhaps, the letter suggested, the chance of the yellow fever being generated in the city was a lesser calamity than the loss of growth and prosperity by unfounded reports. If the doctor were wrong, and the gigantic evil he had created were imaginary, what punishment would he deserve for his whimsical theory?

After that Cobbett said he would drop the whole subject. He inserted a notice in the paper saying that if he used all the pieces he received in the war of the physicians and their partisans, he would not have a single inch of space left for other matters. He called a halt, except to give any gentleman who had been attacked by name in his paper a chance to defend himself. Then the book on the subject would be closed.

Rush went his way, taking care of the sick.

Rush dreaded the prospect of another yellow-fever epidemic. Such catastrophes brought no financial reward, but only heartache, uncertainty, discouragement. He could not charge the poor, even for the medicines he distributed. The danger to his own health, his life, grew as he became older. If the doctor's position already caused him anxiety, a new epidemic could bring final disaster to him and his family.

The Rushes had seven children at this time, varying in age from John at twenty to baby Samuel, age two. Four others had died in infancy. Dr. Rush's family responsibilities were heavy, his expenses ran high.

When yellow fever came again, Julia Rush begged her husband to leave the city. He should not risk another epidemic. Mary, his daughter of thirteen, joined her mother's entreaty. "Father, you almost died before. Please, we'll all go away together—"

The doctor's brows knitted. He frowned easily nowadays. He replied, "If I thought that by remaining I should certainly die, I would still think it my duty to stay." He saw the tears in Mary's eyes. "I will not quit," he added more softly.

Mary did cry. But Julia never failed to understand her husband, whether she thought he was right or wrong. In this case, she could only wish he would do what she urged, for her sake as well as his.

In September the fever took a sharp turn for the worse. The disease appeared more deadly and malignant than in 1793. It struck faster, and with such force that in a

129

short time body functions were beyond being saved by either Rush's depleting methods or the alternative stimulating ones. Among the earliest of the thousand persons to die in this epidemic was a doctor, a patient of Rush.

Nicholas Way, a physician from Wilmington, had been one of Rush's lifelong friends. When he caught the fever in Philadelphia, Rush prescribed for him the usual purges and bleeding. But on the second day of his illness, Dr. Hugh Hodge called on Way.

Ever since 1793 Hodge had been one of those opposed to Dr. Rush. The former relationship, when Hodge called in Rush in a futile attempt to save his dying daughter, had evaporated in the bitter controversies of the first epidemic. Now Hodge examined Dr. Way, told him he had no fever at all, and advised against further bloodletting. However, it was characteristic of the yellow fever that on the second day—which coincided with Hodge's visit—a temporary remission of fever occurred. Notwithstanding Hodge's advice, Dr. Way was bled again, and then, of his own accord and not by Rush's or any other physician's prescription, he took an excessive amount of mercury purging medicine. The doctor died. Hodge instantly announced, publicly, that Rush's overbleeding had killed Dr. Way.

Hodge's charge hurt. Rush had been grieved enough at the loss of his friend as well as patient. Carefully he recorded the case in his *Medical Observations*. He wrote also to the Reverend Ashbel Green, minister of the Second Presbyterian Church, absolutely denying Hodge's accusation. In six bleedings, Rush said, Dr. Way lost "but between forty and forty-five ounces of blood, a quantity by far too little to kill any person (as Dr. Hodge informed you) of Dr. Way's habit of body and force of disease." Hodge's opinion of the cause of death, having seen the
130

patient only once, was "rash and cruel in the highest degree."

Yet Rush made a grave error, perhaps of judgment, or perhaps merely a misprint due to his distressed state of mind. He added in his letter that "from the doctor's size, he could not have had less than 400 ounces of blood in his body in his ordinary health. In the beginning of disease, this quantity is often increased by the sudden stoppage of all the excretions."

The average human body contains about one hundred and seventy to two hundred ounces of blood. The maximum amount in rarest cases is variable, depending upon how much excess liquid the body can produce to replace lost blood. Granted that Dr. Way could have been a very big man, still Rush appears to have been wrong in his estimate by a substantial percentage.

Through a curious turn of affairs William Cobbett had also visited Dr. Way during his illness. He knew the exact story as told by Way himself before he died. He waited nearly a month before he said anything, and then, selecting the end of one of his vicious attacks on Rush, Cobbett published the facts as he knew them. He reported Dr. Way's own overdose of mercury, and concluded with an odd sense of justice: "I think Dr. Rush exempt from blame in the case of Way."

Still another physician friend of Rush came down with the disease. The illness of young Dr. Physick nearly coincided with Way's. But Physick recovered. Afterward he had this testimonial printed in the *United States Gazette:*

> With a view of inspiring confidence in blood-letting in the cure of yellow fever, I take this method of informing my fellow citizens that I lost during my last attack of that fever a hundred and seventy-six

ounces of blood by twenty-two bleedings in ten days. The efficacy of this invaluable remedy was aided by frequent and copious evacuations from my bowels, and a moderate salivation.

He was deeply grateful to Dr. Rush.

The fever continued to increase in violence through that September of 1797. Philadelphia again took on the aspect of a desolated city, with thousands of its people having fled and the rest keeping indoors as much as possible. Yellow flags hung at the doors of infected houses, and carts with the dead rolled day and night through the streets. The doctors, twenty-four of them in the city normally between forty and fifty thousand, struggled to stop the rising flood of disease. Of these twenty-four doctors, eight caught the fever. Rush in his office at home and with his horse and carriage outside carried on tirelessly as he had in 1793.

Then all at once the thunderbolts were unleashed at Benjamin Rush's head.


## 17    "The Times Are Ominous Indeed"

WHAT prompted the attack against Benjamin Rush at this particular moment was a basic question confronting the judges and jury two years later in Pennsylvania's Supreme Court. At the trial the prosecution attempted to show by evidence what was in Cobbett's mind. For one example, it was proven that a few days after Rush delivered his eulogium on Rittenhouse, Dr. William Dewees was at Cobbett's house. Dewees, Rush's friend, asked Cobbett if he had heard the eulogium. No, Cobbett replied, but he had read it. How did he like it, Dewees could not resist asking. Dr. Rush, Cobbett said, should have confined himself to medicine and let politics alone. He added angrily to Dewees, "Damn him, I will attack him for it!"

132

The eulogium was "too republican" for him, Cobbett told Dewees.

But Cobbett insisted afterward that his attacks on Rush's medical theories had nothing to do with the eulogium threat. He had, Cobbett said, already dispatched the eulogium in January, 1797. His writings against the yellow-fever treatment were only for the public good, he stated.

The first blow did not come from Cobbett at all. It appeared in the *United States Gazette,* the newspaper which, only several days before this time, had published Dr. Physick's testimonial on bloodletting. John Fenno, friend of Alexander Hamilton, had originally started his paper in New York under Hamilton's blessing. It continued in Philadelphia practically as the official organ of the Federalist party.

Fenno began by attacking Rush's "lunatic system of medicine." The doctor, he declared, had acquired the idea of bloodletting from the French Revolution.

Almost as if on cue, Cobbett picked up the attack. On Monday, September 18, *Porcupine's Gazette* published a facetious and fictitious letter signed by "A Tavern Keeper." It described the plight of the poor tavern keeper who found out that his business had been ruined by the prevailing sickness. In the solitude of his deserted barroom he had time to read the soporific essays of the scribbling physicians and their hopeful pupils. He found the whole *Materia Medica* was beautifully reduced to the very simple system of copious bloodletting and comfortable evacuation. He had determined to desert a trade ruined by fever and commence a business which had fever for its support. He observed that innkeeping was analogous to the profession of physicians. Innkeepers certainly were used to evacuations, as the purses of their guests could testify, and they could furnish copious drafts as well as be thoroughly

133

acquainted with the whole system of dieting and mixing compounds. As to bloodletting, their hostlers were experienced, and would be limited to drawing no more blood from the human body than they did from their own horses. As it was necessary to bleed patients until they fainted, innkeepers always had at hand the best cordials to revive them. He had heard that barbers formerly exercised the noble art of phlebotomy, being after that called barber-surgeons. The tavern keeper suggested that his trade take the name of "Vintner-Physicians."

But if the supposed tavern keeper's letter was meant to be sharply humorous, the item that appeared in the following day's edition of *Porcupine's Gazette* was not. No subtlety at all concealed the fury of this new writing:

### MEDICAL PUFFING

The times are ominous indeed,
When quack to quack cries, *purge* and *bleed*.

Those who are in the habit of looking over the gazettes which come in from the different parts of the country, must have observed, and with no small degree of indignation, the arts which our remorseless *bleeder* is making use of to puff off his preposterous practice. He has, unfortunately, his partisans in every quarter of the country. To these he writes letters, and in return gets letters from them; he extols their practice, and they extol his; and there is scarcely a page of any newspaper that I see which has the good fortune to escape the poison of their prescriptions. Blood, blood! still they cry, More blood! In every sentence they menace our poor veins. Their language is as frightful to the ears of the alarmed multitude as is the raven's croak to those of the sickly flock.

Cobbett's article continued by quoting a letter from one Dr. Tilton of Wilmington, addressed to Dr. Rush and endorsing copious bloodletting and mercurial purges. Dr. Tilton, as quoted, advised that mercury was useful not merely as a cathartic but as a "specific against all kinds of
134

*Above,* back of the State House, Philadelphia, 1799

*Below,* Second Street, north from Market Street, with Christ Church, 1799

*Above,* political cartoon of 1795. *Courtesy of the New-York Historical Society, New York City*

*Below,* cartoon of 1798 satirizing members of Congress

Shipyard where the frigate *Philadelphia* was being built in preparation for war with France

Dr. Benjamin Rush

*Right,* David Rittenhouse. The eulogy in his memory delivered by Dr. Rush prompted Cobbett's first diatribe against the famous physician.

*Left,* Dr. Physick, who issued a testimonial ascribing his recovery from yellow fever to copious blood lettings and purges

*Right,* Justice Edward Shippen, the judge who presided at the trial

See Porcupine, in Colours just Portray'd, | Veild in darkness, acts the afsafsins part.
Urg'd by old Nick to drive his dirty trade, | And triumphs much to stab you to the heart.

Cartoon of Peter Porcupine

William Cobbett, alias Peter Porcupine

Pennsylvania Hospital in Philadelphia

contagion," including smallpox, measles, dysentery, and other "contagious" diseases. Cobbett continued his article:

> This Dr. Tilton is a kind of Puritan; a sour, wry-faced, incorrigible democrat. He has the pride of Lucifer himself, and to me it is astonishing that he should have condescended to become the trumpet, the underling, the mere barber-surgeon of the master bleeder.
> The mercurial purges, too, Dr. Tilton must break forth in praise of! Mercury is good for everything that is contagious! Is it good for sansculottism, Doctor? If it be, in the name of goodness, take a double dose of it twice a day till it has wrought a cure. Dr. Rush, in that emphatical style which is peculiar to himself, calls *mercury* "the Samson of medicine." In his hands and those of his partisans, it may indeed be justly compared to Samson; for I verily believe they have slain more Americans with it than ever Samson slew of the Philistines. The Israelite slew his thousands, but the Rushites have slain their tens of thousands.

From that moment Benjamin Rush was kept under savage, remorseless pressure. Fenno continued his tirades in the *United States Gazette*. Even Dr. Currie, as a representative of the medical profession, joined the newspaper attacks against Rush. And Cobbett kept on:

> . . . potent quack . . . bare-faced puff . . . all this bustle of letters and addresses and prescriptions in the name of Dr. Rush is intended to make the duped world believe that he is the oracle at Philadelphia . . . all the other physicians are mere clyster-pipe Dicks under him . . .

The doctor tried to ignore the campaign. His family could not. How Rush first learned of Porcupine's attack can be surmised. Probably he did not subscribe regularly to *Porcupine's Gazette*. He had no time for reading at all during the epidemic, and anyway he must have judged Cobbett's paper as being worth no more than bombastic political rot. Someone must have told him about the article, probably not a patient, but more likely a friend who stopped him in the street and handed him a copy of the paper with a sympathetic grin.

And probably one of the family bought the *Gazette* after that at a local store—his son John, more than likely. The Rushes must have been hypnotized in horror anticipating what Cobbett would come forth with next. When the doctor himself read the articles his knuckles must have tightened in anger. Surely he did feel uneasy about the eventual outcome.

Ignore the attacks as he would, he could not avoid meeting head on the public reaction. No one could be held up to such ridicule without a certain loss of prestige. People stared at him in the streets, suspicions grew. The doctor was being laughed at, but the laughter held a bitter note in the city where yellow fever and death were stalking the population through days and nights unending.

Rush's anger was impotent against Cobbett's savagery. Worse, as the attacks continued, he was seized by desperate panic.

He carried others down with him. Any physician who shared Rush's medical views plus Jefferson's politics was marked as a Cobbett target. One such was a Dr. Michael Leib, formerly an apprentice to Rush and now a Democratic-Republican member of the State Legislature. This combination Cobbett could not miss. Peter Porcupine wrote:

> It is an ill wind that blows nobody any good. One would think that the dreadful disease that afflicts the city at this time, and that has driven away one third of its inhabitants, could not possibly be a source of good for anyone; yet, we see, it has raised Doctor Leib from the dirt into a one-horse chair! . . .
>
> This new-born son of Esculapius, when mounted in his Yellow-Fever equipage, puts one in mind of Racine's description of Death:

"A horrid *grinning* monster,
With steed raw-bon'd and lash tremendous,
Driving his chariot wheels o'er smiling Peace
And rosy Health, and spreading all around
Terror, anguish and despair."

No wonder the inhabitants of Germantown were alarmed.

Rush's colleague of Wilmington, Dr. Tilton, came under attack again, this time as a "self-consequent mercurial ghost . . . a crooked-faced quack, who, when he was called to help a woman suffering from a fall, noticed a bruise on her arm. He immediately pronounced her complaints the yellow fever, made his escape, and has not seen her since."

Another letter by Cobbett's fictitious tavern keeper appeared, this time referring to the tavern keeper's employee, an impudent hostler who knew his business well—particularly the art of bleeding horses. The hostler bought Dr. Rush's book on yellow fever, and after studying it decided to go into the medical business himself. The hostler and the tavern keeper argued about the merits of bloodletting, and the tavern keeper wanted Mr. Porcupine to know he was for the lancet, because dead men never tell tales. The tavern keeper reported that he had got his carriage newly painted, and engaged a new French hostler, "whose merits and *sang froid* in the use of the lancet are, I believe, unrivaled, for I believe he was an *élève* of Robespierre's." Finally the tavern keeper assured Porcupine, "I have also hired a few nurses whose abilities I am well acquainted with. They will never desert their patients as I have engaged to supply them constantly with excellent gin, and have also promised them the pillage of such of my patients as may be determined to die."

The effect on Dr. Rush was cumulative. His reputation in the city shook to its foundations.

The doctor had to force himself to leave the house to face his remaining patients. His pride was shattered. To be held up to ridicule and scorn was galling to any man, but to Rush it was anguish. Besides his long days of work and anxiety he had to bear what he called this overflowing measure of the most merciless persecution. Frantically he protested that he had not merited the indifference with which Philadelphia's citizens watched the butchery of his character.

Dr. Rush was being driven toward the crisis of his life. Yet the yellow fever raged on without abating.

The blows rained on, too. Toward the end of September the tavern keeper's hostler wrote to "Mr. Porcupine." He had quarreled with the tavern keeper, he said. The tavern keeper was both a fool and a devil, a fool for presuming to decide upon the disputes of physicians, and a devil, nay the prince of devils, for ridiculing that godlike philanthropist—meaning Benjamin Rush,

> —that savior of men, whose omniscient soul, whose omnipotent genius discovered this remedy, and whose godlike benevolence industriously, incessantly labored to propagate it for the good of mankind. . . . The tavern keeper ridiculed bloodletting. I recommend it, and how are the poor illiterate to determine what to do? Let them ask the physicians—but they are as much divided as the tavern keeper and myself. One doctor says, If you bleed you will die; another says, You will die if you do not bleed. How then are we to act? . . . The tavern keeper knows that a pig dies by the loss of blood when its carotids are opened; therefore he holds it dangerous to lose blood at all; we vulgar are fools for attempting to reason on a subject we know nothing about. I act as a wise illiterate ought. Facts are my criterion. I see that those only recover who are bled freely, which is sufficient to determine me in favor of bloodletting. Dr. Rush has saved my life by the loss of eighty ounces in one day; therefore, I am an advocate of the lancet, and all the chicanery of all the tavern keepers in Philadelphia shall not proselyte me. The merits of the lancet will be universally ac-

knowledged before many years, in spite of *prejudice, fools, devils.*

The hostler ended by wishing the tavern keeper and all enemies of the lancet no other punishment than a severe attack of yellow fever, with liberty to use the lancet or not. Then the world would either be reformed, he wrote, or freed of all stupid quacks, with free scope given to the sword and the shield as the instruments of health.

Many Philadelphians watched with keen enjoyment this unrelenting torture pressed on Benjamin Rush. A just punishment, they said, for his political principles, his aspersions against the city for being the origin of the fever, for his menacing and dangerous theories of medicine. They prophesied his downfall. Many indeed, even former patients, waited like wolves for the doctor's destruction.

The newspaper vituperation piled higher. Peale's American Museum was in Philadelphia. To Peale, Cobbett addressed an open letter:

> In these degenerate days dog eats dog, and surgeon slays surgeon, when he can get no other subject. Take my advice: throw out your snakes and your alligators, and replace them by the more venomous brutes above mentioned; and be assured that you will no longer stand in need of newspaper puffs; nor will signify a farthing whether your shop be healthy or not. You will have hundreds of customers, though the pestilence should rage all around you, and though Dr. Rush with the lancet in his hand should be your doorkeeper.

Goaded beyond all endurance, Dr. Rush went to see a lawyer. He selected Joseph Hopkinson, whose family had long been patients of the doctor's, and in whom Rush could trust.

Hopkinson was only twenty-seven. He had never tried a really important case. But he had a good background and training. An older man might have refused to take a case with odds so heavily against him.

139

The young lawyer listened carefully. He noticed the doctor's nervous hands, the tension under which he talked. Rush scarcely had to tell his story, for everyone knew it. What he wanted was legal aid for his plans.

Joseph Hopkinson expressed doubt, showing as much consideration as he could for his distraught client. American juries were prejudiced in favor of freedom of the press, he said. Of course, abuse of that freedom by constant slanderous and libelous statements had become all too common. But other court trials had not offered substantial remedy. Dr. Rush would be taking a very great risk by pressing a case. If he lost, his position would be far worse. More than that, the vindictive nature of William Cobbett was too dangerous to tamper with.

No, Rush said. He insisted on proceeding.

Hopkinson agreed at last, but said he would confer with Jared Ingersoll, an older and more experienced lawyer. They would see what they could do.

As a result, Benjamin Rush brought suit, claiming damages for libel, against both William Cobbett and John Fenno. This was the first of October, 1797.

Under the law, Cobbett should have refrained from further attacks pending the outcome of the suit. Rush's action technically restrained both Cobbett and Fenno and should have halted their further persecution.

The effect was quite the reverse. Fenno replied with an angry article on the liberty of the press. He castigated Rush all over again. Cobbett was merely scornful:

> The doctor finds his little reputation as a physician in as dangerous a way as ever a poor yellow fever man was in. We know very well what we ought to do, and if God grants us life, we shall do it completely.

Cobbett nearly did do it completely. "One of the Rushites need be neither a great physician nor a FORTUNE TELLER to predict the exact moment of a patient's decease. All they have to determine is when they shall be at leisure to give him his LAST BLEEDING."

Then, despite this pending suit, Cobbett published in his paper a long analysis of Dr. Rush's behavior in the yellow-fever epidemic of 1793. He ascribed the report to Dr. William Currie. Currie must indeed have supplied the information, for in that disastrous summer of 1793 William Cobbett was tutoring in Wilmington, Delaware. All he knew of the epidemic was hearsay. Yet Cobbett undoubtedly had done much of the writing, for the sharply sardonic style showed the Englishman's masterful hand.

The piece in *Porcupine's Gazette* was headed "Dr. Currie's Account of Rush's Conduct in 1793." It appeared on Saturday, October 7.

Incident by incident, the Cobbett-Currie combination examined Benjamin Rush's connection with the events of 1793. They referred to the newspaper files and the contradictory letters published by the different doctors. They unearthed Rush's correspondence of the time. Mainly, they took Rush's own record of the epidemic as published in his *Observations on the Yellow Fever*. They criticized his claims of cures, ridiculed the debilitating method of treatment he arrived at after so much mental agony. Advertisements he had arranged with the apothecaries for the supply of ten and ten were quoted, and held up to scorn. The results of purging and bleeding which Rush thought he had achieved were called ludicrous exaggerations. "He remembered to forget the victims that were falling by the hands of his apostles," the newspaper article said.

Currie, aided by Cobbett, had this to say about Dr. Benjamin Rush in 1793:

> So much was the Doctor about this period possessed with the notion that he was the only man of common sense existing, that he not only refused to

141

consult with any but his former pupils who submitted to obey his dictates, and rudely intruded his advice upon other people's patients. He also appointed two illiterate Negro men, and sent them into all the alleys and byplaces in the city with orders to bleed and give his sweating purges, as he empirically called them, to all they could find sick, without regard to age, sex or constitution; and bloody and dirty work they made among the poor miserable creatures that fell in their way.

That his mind was elevated to a state of enthusiasm bordering on frenzy, I had frequent opportunity of observing; and I have heard from popular reports that in passing through Kensington one day, with his black man on the seat of his chaise alongside of him, he cried out with vociferation, "Bleed and purge all Kensington! Drive on, boy!"

## *18*   *"Sangrado"*

ON MONDAY, October 16, Porcupine struck with the sharpest quill of all:

### SANGRADO

Who can read the following extract from *Gil Blas* without being tempted to imagine that the author foresaw the person and practice of Rush? "I went to fetch Dr. Sangrado. He was a *tall, pale, hungry-looking fellow* who had kept the shears of Clothos employed for forty years at least. This learned Doctor had a very grave appearance. He weighed his discourse, and *gave vast pomposity to his expressions.* After having looked at my master, he observed, with a doctor-like air, We must, my dear good sir, supply the want of transpiration. Sangrado then sent me for a surgeon whom he named and whom he made draw from my master *six good porringers of blood,* as a beginning to supply the want of transpiration. When this blessed prelude was over, he said to the surgeon, Master Martin Onez, return in three hours' time and take as much more, and tomorrow you'll begin again fresh. *It is a gross error to suppose that blood is necessary to the conservation of life.*

142

And on the following day this further item appeared:

### DYING EASY

> Rush having bled a patient within an inch of the grave, and being about to give him the finishing stroke, the relations remonstrated, observing that it was useless for that the poor young man was already dying: "Very well, then," replied the Quack, "it will *put him out of his misery*, and make him *die easy!*" And ought butchers like this to be tolerated? These monsters look upon every patient that has the misfortune to fall into their hands, as a lump of flesh and blood on which they have a right to make experiments. A modern philosopher cares no more about the life of a man than about the life of a rat or sparrow. I would caution everyone to avoid the bloody race; but let this caution never be neglected *by those who differ from them in politics.*

Dr. Rush cracked. He was ready to give up. Philadelphia, his practice, and the entire business of medicine turned sour. All that he had done, had stood for, had believed in, fell into ashes.

He talked it over with Julia. She shared his feelings. There was one possible way out. It would be hard for both of them, but she urged him to take it.

Dr. Rush wrote to a doctor in New York, a close friend, John Rodgers. He told Rodgers that ever since 1793 he had lived in Philadelphia as he might in a foreign country. It was difficult for him, worse for his family. If it were not for strangers who came as patients, he could not support his family. He would like to move to New York, and leave Philadelphia forever. He wondered, could he get a professor's chair at Columbia University? If so, he would give up active practice altogether. He hoped to live in the country near the University on a place with a garden and pasture. Was there any chance of this proposition succeeding?

To his question came a quick reply. Yes, there certainly was a chance. The medical faculty at Columbia were enthusiastic. One professor offered to resign his own chair to make a place for Rush to teach the practice of medicine. Here was a unique opportunity for the College, they said, and for New York City, too. Unanimously the faculty voted a recommendation that Rush be invited to join them.

Merely as a formality their recommendation had to go before the trustees for routine approval. But—one of the trustees was Alexander Hamilton. He heard the name of Rush. Immediately, at the trustees' meeting, Hamilton protested: the College did not need a new professor. What should have been a pro forma approval turned into a discussion. Hamilton was influential, and adamant. The recommendation was held over for the next meeting.

Rush's friend reported back to him with anger at this turn of events. At the next trustees' meeting the approval would surely go through. Pressure would be brought to bear against Hamilton's opposition.

Weak and weary, Benjamin Rush broke under this last indignity. He replied to Rodgers, "When I proposed removing from Philadelphia to New York, I contemplated a situation in which I could follow the wishes of my heart to live in peace with everybody. . . . In this wish and expectation I perceive by your letter I have been disappointed. I therefore request that you would stop the business in its present stage, and assure the trustees of the University that I shall not accept of the appointment should it be offered to me after the obstacles that have been thrown in the way of it by Mr. Hamilton."

He could not help adding bitterly, "It is particularly gratifying to me to learn that the opposition to my appointment has come from that gentleman."

Help came from another quarter. Benjamin Rush still had friends. One of the best of them through all the years

144

was John Adams, President of the United States. Adams saw the doctor's difficulties. He offered Rush the government job of Treasurer of the Mint. The position carried a salary of twelve hundred dollars a year.

This was salvation. Grateful to the end of his life to his old friend of the Revolution, Rush accepted.

Adams' action was an especially sensitive one. He realized better than anyone else that Rush was of the opposite political party. The President knew the appointment would be much criticized by his supporters. Many other applications for the post were submitted. But years later Adams told Rush, referring to the Mint position, "I gave you nothing. I was Trustee for our country. Had I known a man more fit, more deserving, you would not have been selected."

For the time being, Cobbett, Fenno, Hamilton, and the legion of Rush's enemies had won. It did not matter so much, after all, for the doctor at least had a certain amount of financial security. He could regain some of his confidence. He still had spirit to fight on.

On a Monday afternoon in the middle of November, William Cobbett set his copy for the next day's issue. The New York mail came in, and Cobbett glanced swiftly through several newspapers for anything of interest from that city. Suddenly an item caught his attention:

> This day there is to be a meeting of the Trustees of Columbia College. The object of their meeting is to invite Dr. Benjamin Rush to a professorship of the practice of physick in Columbia College. A correspondent is happy in remarking that there are few obstacles in a choice which must result in so many advantages to Columbia College. He is a man born to be useful to society.

Cobbett grinned. He clipped out the item, and with a pen underlined the sentence, "He is a man born to be

145

useful to society." On a piece of paper he wrote the following comment:

"And so is a mosquito, a horse-leech, a ferret, a polecat, a weazel: for these are all bleeders, and understand their business full as well as Dr. Rush does his."

Cobbett sniffed. He called one of his men over to him. "Put this in for tomorrow's *Gazette*," he said.


## 19   *Porcupine's Gazette*

THE publishing shop in the house on Second Street was a busy place. Three thousand copies of *Porcupine's Gazette* were printed and distributed each day. Local news around the city, developments in Federal and state governments, personal items came in a steady stream. With each mail from abroad foreign news reports arrived.

The newspaper's publisher received this mass of information, sorted and digested it, rewrote into readable form the items which he considered newsworthy. At his writing table William Cobbett governed the businesss details of his newspaper, and wrote articles—or editorials—on his interpretations of current personalities and events. Besides all this, his bookstore did a good business.

Cobbett was stockier than ever as one might have seen him sitting at his table. He moved and spoke deliberately, turned sharp when aroused. In what he said, as in the way he moved, he was emphatic. Well dressed, as suited his present circumstances, he presented a picture of an efficient man running an efficient establishment.

Benjamin Rush was not the only American to feel the weight of Porcupine's assaults. By potshot and heavy barrage he kept under fire the entire Democratic-Republican faction, and singled out party leaders and any

146

who had the temerity to identify themselves with republicanism. With blasting adjectives, sly slurs, and knife-edged personal quips he wielded the power of his newspaper to shift the balance of American attitudes.

He maintained persistent attacks on Franklin Bache, as spokesman for the Democratic-Republican party, describing him as an ill-looking devil whose eyes never got above his knees, with sallow complexion, hollow cheeks, dead eyes, and the general appearance of a fellow who had been about a week or ten days on a gibbet.

By 1797 Cobbett's goal came within reach. The whole aspect of international relations was changing: the Jay Treaty eased tension with the British while at the same time relations with France deteriorated. Now French raids on American shipping were arousing public indignation. Instead of the former anti-British expressions, rumbles of anger swung toward France.

These were turns of history. They suited Cobbett's purpose exactly. He made the most of them, fostered them by every possible means.

Cobbett had started on his career in a city where an Englishman was ashamed to acknowledge his own country. He lived there long enough to see Philadelphians celebrate a victory of Lord Nelson over the French and to be serenaded himself with "God Save the King." What a change, he remarked. Certainly not *entirely* to be ascribed to him, he added modestly.

"But"—using Cobbett's own description of himself—"it was a change which I had a considerable share in producing; I stayed the mischief; I prevented that which would have prevented us from profiting from the events which time was hastening along. My American friends gave me all the credit for this change; I claim no such thing; but I know that I deserve, and that I shall have, the lasting gratitude of both countries."

Porcupine's victims usually suffered in silence. Freedom of the press in America was a sacrosanct citadel which few dared invade. Under its protection the most defamatory remarks could be published in public print, and juries were in no mood to stop the practice for fear of restraining freedom of expression. This liberty of publication was Cobbett's safeguard.

He was challenged seriously only twice—once by the Spanish minister to the United States, and the second time by Benjamin Rush's pending lawsuit.

Porcupine's onslaught against His Catholic Majesty, Charles IV, King of Spain, was one of his most dramatic campaigns. Spain, though a monarchy, had allied itself with revolutionary France. The Spanish minister to the United States, Chevalier Charles de Yrujo, took up the cause of the French during his residence in Philadelphia. He became notoriously involved in the cloudy circles of international intrigue in the nation's capital, and at once made himself a major target for Peter Porcupine.

Porcupine loosed his quills at the King of Spain. He referred to Charles as the degenerate prince who swayed the Spanish scepter, whom the French kept on the throne merely as a trophy of their power or as the butt of their insolence. He seemed destitute not only of the dignity of a king but of the common virtues of a man, Porcupine wrote. Not content with allying himself to the French murderers of their own benevolent king, he had become the subtle tool of all their most nefarious politics.

The minister's turn came next in Cobbett's columns. Referring to De Yrujo, Porcupine declared that as the sovereign is at home, so is the minister abroad. The one was governed like a dependent by the nod of the despots of Paris, and the other by the direction of the French agent in America.

William Cobbett maintained a consistent and drumming barrage at the Spanish, lasting for some length of time. The minister was outraged. He complained to the United States Secretary of State. The Attorney General finally began proceedings against Cobbett for libel.

This action in itself was a contradiction for the government, under the current Federalist administration. Only the necessity of diplomatic courtesy and technicality would have brought the unwilling Federalists to prosecute the publisher who spoke for their own party.

Perhaps De Yrujo realized this. The case dragged in Federal Court. The Spanish minister insisted on fast action. He sought it in the state courts of Pennsylvania, politically more liberal toward republican causes. . . .

On Saturday, November 18, 1797, at precisely noon, a knock sounded on William Cobbett's door. The sheriff of Philadelphia County presented himself.

"Mr. Cobbett," he said, "I must tell you that I am ordered to take you under arrest before the Court at half-past one today."

Cobbett looked up from his work with amazement. "What in God's name is this?" he wanted to know.

The sheriff produced his warrant. He was to bring William Cobbett, printer and publisher of "certain infamous and wicked libels" against the King of Spain and his envoy, at the designated time before the Chief Justice of Pennsylvania.

"But I have already given bond in Federal Court for this same thing," Cobbett protested.

"I wouldn't know about that, sir."

"You said half-past one? I'm given one hour and a half to produce bail? Infamous!"

"I am sorry, sir."

Cobbett frowned. He glanced at the warrant again. It was signed by Thomas McKean, Chief Justice, one of his newspaper victims. McKean, strong Jeffersonian, active in the Revolution, signer of the Declaration, had been Chief Justice of Pennsylvania for twenty years. Cobbett had persistently denounced him for his politics.

Unlike the Federal government, the government of Pennsylvania was primarily Democratic-Republican, and a curse to Cobbett.

Cobbett's eyebrows lifted contemptuously. "Very well," he said to the sheriff. "I will tell my wife first. Then I will find someone to furnish the bail. The judge, I believe, will be disappointed that I have friends to help me!"

He called on his friend Benjamin North, a Philadelphian who had the warmest regard for William Cobbett. North came to his rescue promptly, and arranged that bail be furnished.

Punctually at one-thirty Cobbett went before Judge McKean in his study. The November day was cold, and a fire burned in the fireplace. "Please sit down, Mr. Cobbett," the judge said. He himself sat on the opposite side of the fire. For a time the judge spoke of minor things, occasionally scrutinizing Cobbett. Then he took up a file of newspapers.

"Mr. Cobbett, I will ask you to look at these. Did you print and publish them?"

"The law does not require me to answer any questions in this stage of the business," Cobbett told him coldly. "Therefore, I will not reply."

"What, sir? You won't answer?" The judge grew purple. "Get off that chair and stand before me!"

"Yes, sir, but it was you asked me to sit down."

"Never mind that. I bind you over to the Grand Jury. That will be all, Mr. Cobbett."

That was indeed about all, for on December 7 the Grand Jury in Philadelphia by a vote of ten to nine released Cobbett from the charges. They returned the bill of indictment "Ignoramus," meaning "we do not know" that the evidence was sufficient for a true bill of indictment.

Then in Federal Court the same thing happened. In both cases the juries were unwilling to indict the Porcupine.

William Cobbett was free to carry on with stinging effect his verbal war against Spain, the government of France, anti-British republicans, and Jeffersonians whether they were members of Congress, judges, or doctors.

The case brought by Dr. Rush was hanging in the air. Cobbett had no intention of worrying about that. The Spanish case had set a precedent.

"We have often been told," he wrote in his newspaper in a mood of annoyance, "in a silly, vaunting strain that we alone enjoy the real liberty of the press, and that *truth* is not a libel here as it is in Britain. Well: now I take upon me to assert that the press is, both in law and in practice, a thousand times freer in Britain than it is in this country; and this assertion I pledge myself to make good against any facts or arguments that can be brought to oppose it. There's my gauntlet, citizens. After so much boasting there will certainly be somebody found to take it up."

Yes, somebody was taking up Mr. Cobbett's gauntlet —none other than that Dr. Rush whom he considered so preposterous. But the doctor's way of doing it was scarcely in the manner in which Cobbett's challenge was intended.

Liberty of the press—so much discussed—required a clear-cut definition of meaning.

Rush dropped the suit against John Fenno, on advice of counsel that he had too little chance to win against the American publisher. He would not heed similar advice on Cobbett. That battle had to be fought through to the end.

151

At stake was not only Rush's own reputation but also countless lives which would be lost if the opposition in medicine prevailed.

Because of delays and postponements, it was exactly two years before the case came to trial.

## 20   *A Horse for Cobbett*

WILLIAM COBBETT left Philadelphia for New York five days before the trial began on Friday, December 13, 1799. He moved out with his family from the city of his triumph, an angry, petulant man.

The change in his affairs came suddenly.

As a meteor burns brightest the moment before its disintegration, so Cobbett flamed into that year 1799. His newspaper, his pseudonym of Porcupine were at the peak of public influence. Cobbett at the beginning of the year was indeed coming remarkably close to shaping the whole United States to his pattern.

The man who did most to stop him was himself a Federalist—John Adams, President of the United States.

What Adams did to Cobbett was merely a coincidence in the unfolding events. The famous "X Y Z Affair" of 1798 infuriated all America against the French. It was the result of the repudiation by the government in Paris of the American emissaries sent over to settle differences. The initials were nicknames of three French officials who offered insulting terms for a settlement—the demand for a government loan, and a bribe before negotiating any treaty. Relations with France were at low ebb. The "undeclared war" at sea began in 1798 with the French capture of an American schooner.

In Philadelphia the Hamilton group used the occasion to demand an all-out declaration of war. Patriotic
152

fervor swept through the country. Militias were organized, the United States Navy was established, the army enlarged, George Washington made commanding officer again with Alexander Hamilton himself next in rank. Throughout the nation the popular cry to Congress was for "War with France!"

The Alien and Sedition Acts were passed by Federalists in Congress, enabling the administration to deport undesirable aliens, to quash threats of insurrection, and to punish false and malicious writings against the government, Congress, or the President. Under the Sedition Act ten Democratic-Republican editors and publishers were convicted for protesting against anti-French measures.

It had been an amazing about-face for Americans in the five years since 1794. When William Cobbett first began to write on politics in Philadelphia, Great Britain was the arch villain, the object of hate. France in the throes of revolution had the bulk of American sympathy. By 1799 all that was exactly reversed. The Jay Treaty and greater mutual respect had eased Anglo-American relations. The French, on the other hand, were bitter about American neutrality in their war with England. They repudiated their friendship and close ties to the United States. American national pride was provoked.

William Cobbett rode the tide of French unpopularity. More than that, he pushed it along perhaps more than any other single man could do. His newspaper columns condemned the French, pointed out the dangers of French invasion, and the bloody results if their barbarian soldiers landed on American shores. He reported military news, and his headlines screamed for "War!"

It was Hamilton's policy to want a French war, and Cobbett's policy, too. War against France ought not only to bring vengeance on the republicans of the French Revolution but must inevitably bring the United States

153

into close alliance with Great Britain. Cobbett might even yet have been dreaming of the restoration of the monarchy over the former colonies.

But then John Adams stood out for himself. In the face of his own party he made a cautious overture toward peace. In spite of his own cabinet he proposed to the Senate the nomination of a new minister to Paris, as the first move for peaceful negotiations.

Cobbett was horrified. This was miscarriage of all his plans. He could not believe at first that Adams would take such a step. Finally he declared that the President was a traitor to his cause and party.

Now Porcupine was in trouble. Adams repudiated the Hamilton faction altogether, eventually threw its representatives in his cabinet out of office. Popular sympathy changed again. War threats subsided. The Federalists were split and the Democratic-Republicans gained. Almost overnight William Cobbett was left holding an empty bag —or rather an aimless newspaper.

Worse, an angry President Adams considered deporting him under the same Alien and Sedition Acts which had been aimed against the French.

Cobbett lost in local Pennsylvania politics, too. Thomas McKean, the judge who was on the worst terms with Cobbett, ran for the governorship. Cobbett promised publicly, "I will never live six months under his sovereign sway. As soon as he is safe in his saddle, I shall begin to look for a horse."

McKean did win. Cobbett wrote a sneering admission of defeat for his cause: "The election of my *Democratic Judge* as Governor of Pennsylvania, undeniably the most influential state in the Union, has in my opinion *decided* the fate of what has been called Federalism." He added that McKean's selection would be the "onset in a struggle

154

which will terminate in the complete triumph of Democracy."

According to his promise, it was time for him to look
for a horse.

Toward the end of 1799 William Cobbett said to his
wife, "I have talked of moving to New York. The time
has come. We will open up a new bookshop there."

"What of Dr. Rush's lawsuit?" Nancy asked. "Didn't
you say—"

Cobbett flexed his heavy fingers. "What of it?" he
demanded. "I trust my lawyers. Perhaps I shall lose, but
they have no power really to hurt me in Philadelphia.
What can they do?" He paused for a moment. "There will
be no more *Porcupine's Gazette*," he told her. "Nancy,
we shall have a hard time for a while in New York."

She laughed softly. "You know I will love you through
any kind of fortune, whether good or bad."

He lifted his hands and looked at them. "I have found
out in Philadelphia how much I can do, and how to do
it," he said. He straightened his broad shoulders. "The rest
of the world has only seen the beginning of me, my dear!"

# The Trial

## 21

## *"Slander Is a Headlong Torrent"*

THE trial before the State Supreme Court moved on through the morning.

Joseph Hopkinson's opening address to the jury on behalf of his client lasted nearly two hours. He ranged from the definitions of slander to a comparison of press freedom between the United States and England—a subject on which Cobbett had often expressed himself in terms disproving his own contention that America offered no liberty.

"Slander is a headlong torrent that rushes over the land," Rush's counsel cried. "Like a mighty water rolling from the mountain's top, it spreads and strengthens as it goes. Nothing is so high that it cannot reach, or so mean it will not descend to it. Let not the great promise themselves security in the unblemished dignity of their characters, nor the humble expect safety in their obscurity. Like death it comes to every man's door.

"Gentlemen, there are few characters so pure and so impenetrable as to receive the constant, unceasing attack of

159

malicious slander without stain or injury. A physician's reputation is a fabric delicate as air. The slightest gust of popular prejudice or caprice dissipates it, even suspicion destroys it. If he is distrusted he is ruined.

"It is not, gentlemen, this single paragraph or that one that carries with it deadly weight and brings the intended victim to the ground. It is a regular concerted system of defamation, an uninterrupted and persevering attack of calumny and scurrility in every form which they can assume. Sometimes it is made under some dark, mysterious paragraph, and sometimes in the open language of denunciation. Now fear is alarmed with a bold assurance of danger, and then ridicule is exacted by the point of jest. Thus a net is thrown out for every weakness, passion, or prejudice that is afloat in the community, and few escape the entanglement. This, gentlemen, is what scribblers call *writing a man down,* and it is a most abominable species of assassination."

Now Hopkinson led up carefully to one of the main points of the plaintiff's suit, the alleged reason for Cobbett's campaign of slander.

"From what motive or inducement has William Cobbett made his attack—was it a desire to inform the public mind? The nature of the publications shows this was not the case. It does not consist of any examination of the system and principles of Dr. Rush's practice but merely of violent or low personal abuse. Gentlemen, we shall be able by the light of living testimony to trace the low malice of the defendant to personal ignorance, grounded on political prejudice.

"You may remember that some time past a eulogium was delivered, by direction of the Philosophical Society, on the late David Rittenhouse, and that this eulogium was delivered by Dr. Rush. Here, then, originated Cobbett's resentment against Dr. Rush. We shall show you that from

160

that moment he was determined on the attack. Long he waited for an opportunity to gratify this groveling resentment, and discharge the venom that rankled in his heart."

Drawing his hands from the folds of his robe, Hopkinson pounded one palm with his fist. His voice rose angrily:

"When trumpets agitate the ocean to its foundations and rock it in convulsions, numerous noxious animals are thrown up which would otherwise never have seen the light. So in a troubled state of things, wretches are cast up from the very dregs and slime of the community who, in more happy times, would have lived and rotted in obscurity.

"What is so pure, or what so sacred that it has escaped this cormorant of defamation? He has assumed a haughty and tyrannical jurisdiction over everything public or private, political or domestic, religious or moral, not only within the United States but in every quarter of the globe. His arrogant vanity is as disgusting as his crimes are detestable. William Cobbett is indeed a phenomenon even in the courts of defamation!"

Hopkinson reverted to Rush's work during the 1793 epidemic. "Twice he found himself languishing on the bed of sickness," he said, "gasping at the gates of death, distant from his family and almost deserted by every friend. Scarcely had he recovered strength to move when he resumed his dangerous duties. Often did he totter into the infected chambers of the sick when he could not ascend to them without stopping to recover his exhausted strength. It was for the poor and helpless that he thus exposed himself to destruction. The rich had generally fled. How like is this to the conduct of Hippocrates? I wish I could add how like is Philadelphia to Athens. Athens heaped honors and wealth on her physician. But defamation has been the reward of ours.

161

"Let the father of a family assert his honor, that it not descend as a shame upon his children. Let the husband preserve the tender feelings of a wife from insult and her affection from the deep wounds of public reproach. On this high and dignified ground Dr. Rush stands before you."

Rush stirred uncomfortably. This mention of his wife and children was flung at the spectators as well as the jury with what did not seem to him to be dignity. He imagined the stares of the audience at the back of his head. Some of the jurors glanced at him.

Most of the jurors in the box he knew at least slightly. Their faces were stoical as they listened to Joseph Hopkinson's arguments. They seemed particularly impressed with the duty it was theirs to fulfill.

The twelve jurymen were all Philadelphian tradesmen. Included were Isaac Paxton, hardwareman; William Jolly, ironmonger; Joseph Lewis, merchant; Isaac Austin, watchmaker; Thomas Armat, shopkeeper at whose store Rush often dealt; George Thompson, shopkeeper, too; Jacob Sperry, Jr., looking-glass man; John Taggart, merchant; William Roberts, house carpenter; Archibald Bingham and Jacob Rees, both shopkeepers; one Benjamin Garrigues, grocer.

"This day we are to know whether character is deemed a valuable and sacred possession among us," Hopkinson was going on, "in which we have a perfect and inviolable right, or whether it is to be the sport and plaything of malicious ridicule and vulgar wit, the undefended victim of assassinating malevolence. When an offender is found hardy enough to assault the sacred fortress of *reputation* and strive to prostrate it in the dust, hardy enough to brave the vengeance denounced against him by God and man, he should be struck with dreadful and speedy justice,

162

and stand a blighted picture of ruin and infamy. Such an offender, we assert, is William Cobbett, and if such an offender we show him to be, we trust that such a punishment awaits him!"

Rush's chief counsel reached the conclusion of the case's opening speech.

"Virtue, bleeding at every pore," he cried, "calls for justice on her despoiler, and the anxious heart of every honest man pants with impatience to meet in you, *the defenders of virtue and the scourgers of vice!*"

## 22 "I Will Persecute Him While Living, and His Memory After His Death"

JOSEPH HOPKINSON finished. He pulled a handkerchief from under his robes and glanced around the crowded courtroom as if half expecting applause. Then he walked reluctantly back to the counsel table.

The spectators stirred. A common thought ran through the minds of those listening—that Dr. Rush's lawyers had assumed a large burden to prove the statements Hopkinson had made. They waited.

Supporting the young lawyer for Rush were William Lewis, senior attorney of the Philadelphia bar, Moses Levy, and Jared Ingersoll, dry, solemn, and enormously respected.

Opposing them, for William Cobbett, were William Rawle, considered one of the ablest and most careful lawyers practicing, Edward Tilghman, and Robert Goodloe Harper. Harper, representative to Congress from South Carolina and member of the Federalist party, had been one of Cobbett's closest political friends. Harper's life was

163

to be distinguished particularly for giving the name "Liberia" to the republic in Africa established for the settlement of freed American slaves.

Moses Levy moved out now before the bench. He bowed. "With your Honors' leave we will call our first witness."

"Dr. James Mease," the clerk cried.

From among the first rows of spectators Dr. Mease arose and walked across to the witness chair. If he seemed nervous, that was natural for a medical man so out of his element. Rush watched closely the face of his friend.

The witness seated himself, and was sworn by the clerk. According to English law procedures still in use, Dr. Mease had made out a written deposition in advance of these court proceedings. He would be cross-examined after the reading of the deposition. Mr. Levy stood in front of Dr. Mease, holding a paper in his hand. "Sir," he asked, "will you please examine this document?"

The doctor took it, scarcely looked at it. "Yes, sir."

"Is this your deposition regarding the defendant in this case, William Cobbett?"

"Yes, sir."

"Will you be good enough to read the deposition for the benefit of the jury, Dr. Mease?"

The doctor settled himself more firmly in the chair, cleared his throat.

" 'I depose, on oath, that about the middle of April, last year—1798—while I resided at the Marine Hospital, Mr. Cobbett came down to the hospital with a Captain Younghusbands who came to see a man that was landed from on board his ship, with a chronic disease. While the captain went to see the man, Mr. Cobbett remained in the parlor with me. Conversation was introduced between us about Dr. Rush's dispute with Cobbett. The defendant rose

164

upon his feet, and with much warmth said, *"Damn him, he had better withdraw his cause."* I believe that the defendant clinched his fist, and he did appear much agitated. He continued to me—*"or I will persecute him while living, and his memory after death."* When I heard this from the defendant, I told him he was very wrong in his attacks upon Dr. Rush's methods of treatment, for I, Dr. Mease, was a living witness of its efficiency. I said that in my practice I had found it, under Providence, the means of saving hundreds, and I believe thousands had been saved by the mode of treatment recommended by Dr. Rush.' "

Mease finished and handed the paper back to the lawyer.

"Did he repeat these words more than once?" Mr. Levy asked.

"Upon my telling him he was wrong, he repeated, *'Damn him, let him withdraw his cause.'* "

"Did Mr. Cobbett go into any discussion of the propriety, or impropriety, of the medical practice?"

"No."

"That will be all, thank you, Dr. Mease."

The opposition did not question him. Mease went back to his seat.

"Our next witness, your Honors—"

"Dr. William Dewees," the clerk called.

He, too, was sworn and asked to read his deposition. Dewees was the physician, a specialist in obstetrics, whom Dr. Physick had cured of apoplectic fever in a few hours by drawing seventy-five ounces of blood at one time.

" 'This is my deposition, on oath. I declare that a few days after Dr. Rush had delivered his eulogium to the memory of Dr. Rittenhouse, I happened to be at the house of Mr. Cobbett. I asked him if he had heard the eulogium. Mr. Cobbett answered no, but said he had read it. "Did you like it?" I asked. He answered, *"The doctor had better have confined himself to medicine, and let politics alone."* Then I asked, *"What part of it displeased you?"* On which Mr. Cobbett ran upstairs, and brought down the book containing the published eulogium. He showed me the passage he disliked, but I cannot now recollect what it was. Having read it to me, Mr. Cobbett said, *"Damn him, I will attack him for it."* He did not say in what view, or to what effect he would attack him.' "

The instant he finished, all three of the defendant's counsel jumped to their feet. The Honorable Mr. Harper came at Dewees with a quick question.

"Referring to that statement of Mr. Cobbett's," he asked, "did you not understand him to mean that Dr. Rush had advanced some political opinions which he would attack, and endeavor to overthrow?"

"I thought he meant he would attack him on account of his principles. He gave me to understand that the complexion of it was *'too republican'* for him—this was his own phrase."

Mr. Ingersoll came up, for Rush.

Ingersoll:    In the division of opinions among gentlemen of your profession in this city, is Dr. Rush one of those who are for the free use of the lancet?

Witness:    Yes.

Ingersoll:    Of which class have you yourself been?

Witness:    With that of Dr. Rush.

Ingersoll:    Who was William Cobbett's family physician?

Witness:    I cannot tell. I attended his family myself, though never in the yellow fever.

Joseph Hopkinson interrupted. "Did you use Dr. Rush's practice in Mr. Cobbett's family?"

Witness:    Yes.

166

At that statement a murmur ran through the court-room. Mr. Ingersoll resumed.

Ingersoll:    Is that practice or system confined to the dis-ease called the yellow fever?

Witness:    By no means.

This time it was Rawle, for the defense, who broke into the proceedings. "How long did you attend Mr. Cobbett's family?"

Witness:    From the return of the citizens to Philadelphia in 1798. That would be in the autumn, after the fever outbreak of that year.

Mr. Rawle sat down.

Ingersoll:    Have you ever been recommended by Mr. Cobbett to any other families since that period?

Witness:    Yes, frequently.

Another murmur rose from the spectators. Justice Shippen touched his gavel. Then the justice himself asked a question. "I would like an explanation of the meaning of 'the free use of the lancet.' Gentlemen, could you supply a definition?"

Ingersoll:    It is one method of treatment of diseases, your Honor, as compared to other methods not using venesection.

Harper:    It means an indiscriminate use of the lancet.

Hopkinson:    I object to Mr. Harper's use of the term *indiscriminate,* your Honor. *Free* use is not *indiscriminate* use. There is a great difference in the words.

Ingersoll:    Dr. Dewees, will you explain to the Court your understanding of "free use of the lancet"?

Witness:    I would say it was wherever the use of the lancet was necessary, as in inflammatory cases.

167

Justice Shippen: Thank you.

Ingersoll:    Dr. Dewees, you adopted Dr. Rush's system generally?

Witness:    Yes.

Ingersoll:    That will be all, Doctor.

The following witness to be called was John Coxe, Rush's apprentice in 1793, now twenty-six and a graduate M.D.

" 'I depose on oath that on the second of October, 1797, a gentleman who had just arrived from the West Indies called on me. After some conversation he told me he was soon going to sail for England, but before he went he wished to see Peter Porcupine, who had rendered himself so celebrated. He asked me to inform him where Peter Porcupine lived. At that point I accompanied him to the defendant's house myself, having occasionally been in the habit of stepping into his bookstore. After some general conversation had passed between the three of us, I expressed to the defendant my disapprobation of his recent publications respecting the use of the lancet, and respecting Dr. Rush in particular. I said that this remedy had been recommended in certain cases by myself, too. The defendant replied to my observation that his writing could be of very little consequence, or have no effect upon the public mind. I replied that I thought it was impossible that he should imagine what he said was true, for he must know that all he wrote had a very considerable effect, particularly at that time when the mind of the public was so distracted by the fever. He replied as before, adding that as he was not a physician people would naturally suppose that he knew nothing of the subject. I observed to him then that the effect was certainly produced. He replied that he did not believe he should ever have said so much on bleeding or mercurials, if Dr. Rush had not been the author of the system.' "

168

Rush noticed Justice Shippen making a quiet note after Coxe's last sentence.

No questions were asked of Dr. Coxe by either side.

Joseph Hopkinson returned to take the place before the jury box. He held a collection of papers.

"With your Honors' approval," he said, "we wish to present additional evidence of the malicious design and persistence of the defendant. May I read certain passages from *Porcupine's Gazette,* all published after this suit was originally brought by the plaintiff against the defendant?"

The lawyer read to the jury from marked copies of Cobbett's paper. The first was dated October 5, 1797, immediately after Rush initiated his suits against Cobbett and Fenno. Cobbett had reprinted Fenno's tirade against the doctor for bringing the lawsuit against him. Cobbett's reprint, with his own comment attached, contained a portion to sum up his own attitude toward the suit: *I shall wait with entire composure the issue of a trial which I have no doubt will complete the downfall of quackery and empiricism, and will at least be valuable in one point of view, as it will serve to show on what ground stands the Liberty of the Press, whether it is in America an empty name or a valuable reality.*

In the issue of October 6 Cobbett had printed the story of a soldier in South Carolina who came down with yellow fever, wandered off in delirium, and was accidentally immersed in tar spilled from barrels on a wharf. He slept in the tar all night, and by morning was found perfectly recovered from the fever. According to the story, the experiment was repeated on others, generally with success. *This seems like an odd kind of remedy,* Cobbett added parenthetically, *but I would rather TAR, even with the addition of FEATHERS, than venture my life against the lancet of Dr. Rush.*

169

In the issue of *Porcupine's Gazette* for October 20, 1797, the following appeared: *If a quack should fill all the papers from Dunkirk to Marseille with his own eulogiums, under the form of letters from correspondents, to establish the bloodletting and drenching system, and should he prosecute a printer for publishing anything to guard the people against his unmerciful lancet and his samsonic powders, he must be a democrat—for all democrats think that the press was only designed for their use.*

The lawyer for the plaintiff folded his newspapers carefully, bowed slightly to the justices on the bench and again to the jury, and returned to the counsel table.

The prosecution had been opened, and the evidence submitted. Now Cobbett's lawyers presented their arguments for the defense. William Rawle was first, opening his part of the case. He was a man of medium height, quiet in appearance, well mannered to the point of fastidiousness. He faced the jury with composure, and began his argument in a pleasant and assured tone of voice.

"I stand up, gentlemen of the jury, much more impressed with the extraordinary and unusual manner with which the gentleman who preceded me has thought proper to open his cause, than with any danger in which my client stands for the accusations on which this prosecution is grounded." It had not fallen to his lot, Rawle said, since he became a lawyer, to hear such ferocious remarks or such strong stigma used on the character of any man as Hopkinson had used in reference to his client, the defendant. "I could not help being struck with the comparison of that address and the publications which it was meant to implicate. In that comparison I declare I can perceive none which deals in so strong epithets—none bordering so much on abuse, as those with which the gentleman has amused you. If it were possible to commit this opening address to paper, there would be no difficulty in dis-
170

criminating which was most deserving the appellation of slander.

"Gentlemen, if you believe the declaration of my opponent, you must be brought to believe William Cobbett to be the most *insignificant* and *worthless reptile* in creation, and that under the shape of a man he has stalked abroad a very monster—that for him, no justice ought to be had—that he is to be expunged from all ranks of society, that he is to remain an eternal mark for hatred, and courts of justice are never to consider him as even the object of mercy! Mercy, that which we all claim seems not to be his due!"

But this was not the way to appeal to the justice of a jury, Rawle claimed. In spite of efforts to excite them against the defendant, every sensation other than strict equity ought to be left at the courtroom door.

Dr. Rush had been made out to be superior to other men, an angel from God, while Mr. Cobbett was nothing but a demon from infernal regions. Dr. Rush was a respectable citizen who had done much good for society, Rawle agreed, but society had rewarded him for it. If this good angel went from door to door during the yellow-fever epidemic, Rawle noted, no doubt he received compensation. To face death was the lot of his profession.

"Gentlemen, to the declaration filed we have pleaded not guilty," Rawle went on. "We are charged with having *maliciously* written such and such things, in order to destroy the good name Dr. Rush has heretofore borne among his fellow citizens. We deny the malicious part of the accusation, and to obtain our right, we put ourselves upon a jury of our country. Unless it can be proved that the publications laid to our charge are of the nature designated, to wit malicious, we are entitled to your acquittal in the action.

"We have heard the testimony of some medical
171

gentlemen alleging that at periods subsequent to this prosecution being entered, the defendant used words tending to show that these publications proceeded from personal malice. To me, the whole of the publications and charges appear to be free from personal, private or domestic malice. How could they issue from personal malevolence? I ask whether it has been proved in any case that Cobbett has endeavored to intermeddle with the family concerns of Dr. Rush? Or whether, on the other hand, the whole of the publications have not been so far justifiable inasmuch as they treated only on a subject of public inquiry?"

Rawle said that there existed no law of the state or general government that restrained a full and free investigation of the merits of any question in which the public was interested. He told the jury that "it is sufficient for the person accused, if he can show that he has not been guilty of untruth nor entered into the family or moral connections of his accuser, to prove that he has only thrown his mite into the public stock of information."

Rawle drove in his points with deliberate emphasis. He built the core of Cobbett's defense by recalling the horror of the 1793 yellow fever, a disease so unknown to Philadelphians that the wisest were at a loss how to act. Notwithstanding different treatments and experiments, one quarter of the people remaining in the city died, he said. He brought back to mind how many publications succeeded that epidemic. Different methods of treatment became a justifiable subject of public discussion. Even between the members of the medical profession, the language used was of the strongest and most acrimonious.

The fever returned in 1797, and with it all the old controversies resumed. Others besides the defendant expressed opinions on yellow-fever treatment. Mr. Cobbett did not assail the private character of Dr. Rush, or meddle with his family concerns. He discussed a public question
172

as others did. "The topics of public discussion," Rawle declared, "were the free use of the lancet and mercurial purges. And who so natural, so likely to be attacked as the person who was well known to be the head of this system of treatment? Hence the name of Dr. Rush, and the use of bleeding and mercury in the yellow fever came into public notice. This certainly gave to Mr. Cobbett the privilege of expressing his opinion.

"Dr. Rush was at that time a very public character, exercising a very important public function. Mr. Cobbett was unquestionably exercising his constitutional right to do at that time what others did, to examine his public transactions, in which the defendant thought he was on the side of humanity. Suppose we see an individual or a number of persons running headlong toward a precipice, shall I be blamed if I say to them, 'Stop. Listen not to the man who advised you to take that road'?"

Rawle read a letter written by Rush in 1798, admitting the uncertainty of any precise method of treatment in all cases of yellow fever. Rush had acknowledged the difficulties physicians had to meet and, as Rawle quoted the letter, "In 1797 he occasionally lost patients even after the application of bleeding and mercurials." Rawle pointed out, therefore, that the new system of treatment was not the infallible cure it was supposed to be.

The defense lawyer repeatedly urged that no *malice* had been intended, and without malice the defendant was not guilty under the law. Malice had not been proven by the opposition. The effort to prove malice by Dr. Dewees' testimony respecting the Rittenhouse eulogium seemed, to Rawle, "very feeble." Furthermore, the plaintiff had not proven any damage, and without proof the jury must find none was sustained.

"Our client is absent," Rawle said in his concluding statement. "He has rested his case with you to give your

173

decision upon his right of publication. We claim that right for him. I think we shall not claim in vain."

## 23  Quack to Quack

BENJAMIN RUSH watched anxiously this finish of Cobbett's opening argument. He could guess nothing from the expressions of the jury. But as William Rawle walked back to the counsel table someone in the audience suddenly hissed. It was a loud, penetrating sound shocking in its implication.

The courtroom was startled. Heads turned, a rustle of whispering went through the crowd. A slight confusion was audible at the door, and in the hall outside someone laughed.

Justice Shippen gave no sign of having heard.

The defense lawyers conferred for a moment. Then Robert Harper advanced to the jury box.

Harper had been retained by William Cobbett partly out of friendship and partly because of the weight of his congressional position. He was a man of thirty-three, suave but sharp, and a highly qualified lawyer. He had a reputation, too, as a brilliant and convincing speaker. This trial would have to be primarily a battle of arguments between lawyers.

Harper began by defining again the issue in this case. The question was not whether the plaintiff was a physician of eminence, a peaceable citizen, a good father or a tender husband. The question was whether, in the publications cited in the declaration and read to the court, the defendant was actuated by a design to injure Dr. Rush in his personal character and as a physician, or to run down and laugh out of countenance a practice which he considered mischievous. The verdict must be based on one of these alternatives or the other.

174

Malice, from the trial standpoint, must be an attempt to injure the plaintiff's personal or professional character. Without malice the act of slander could not be supported. But every man has a right to attack a ruinous system, Harper said, and he who makes the attack is alone the judge. "If I lift my hand against a set of opinions or practices which I hold to be evil to society," Harper argued, "I must first suppose my liberties or privileges or those of society to be in danger before exercising my freedom of opinion."

Did Mr. Cobbett mean to attack Dr. Rush's system, or his personal and professional character, Harper asked. He read again from *Porcupine's Gazette*: " '*The times are ominous indeed, when quack to quack cries purge and bleed!*' "

The words of the hideous couplet again rang out in the courtroom. Dr. Rush moved uneasily. The fantastic rhyme haunted him. Sometimes he wakened at night with the words beating in his ears.

Harper continued with the rest of the article on "medical puffing." The deadly expressions came out one by one: *remorseless bleeder, blood, blood, still they cry, more blood! Master bleeder, mercury the Samson of medicine.* . . .

"Is there anything like slander in that piece?" Harper asked in a grieved tone of voice. "If so, hardly a newspaper printed in the United States but what might be made subject of inquiry by a jury. I do not justify the language," Harper admitted, "but what does it amount to? It calls an eminent physician a remorseless bleeder. What is that? It is that he pursued bleeding too far. But have not some of the most respectable medical men said also that it is remorseless and destructive?

"Whether bleeding in his practice is pushed too far is not a subject of your inquiry. Whether the defendant meant more than to expose that system which was extreme in his view is a proper subject for you. Was it not wrong that a ruinous system should have been persisted in, when human life was so materially connected with it? This was considered so by Mr. Cobbett, and he thought it his duty to expose it. I am well convinced that it was not only unbecoming language but I believe it to be very untrue— but is it slander? No, it is merely unmeaning ribaldry."

Harper looked at his papers again. " *'Blood, blood, they cry more blood!'* " He glanced at the jury. "To be sure this is very hyperbolical, but strip it of its exaggeration and is it not true? Was it not common during that period for these ideas to be reiterated through the papers and the pamphlets of the city day after day? *'The free use of the lancet, the free use of the lancet,'* was constantly repeated by the medical men in favor of that system. As to the epithet of *master bleeder,* I see no harm in its introduction. It is not slander but a high eulogium, raising him to a pre-eminence rather than giving any abuse. Comparing mercury to Samson and speaking of its ravages, I do not see how conceivably it is applicable to Dr. Rush, but rather to the system—and is particularly pointed at the 'Rushites.'

"Is it slander," Harper asked, "to contend in Congress that certain political opinions contribute to the subversion of government, or tend to rob the country? No," he said, "a great distinction is always held between a man personally and his principles. Miserable would be the times if it were not so," Harper cried, "and much more miserable if we were not permitted to question the practice of a physician without being subjected to an expensive action for slander."

Cobbett's writings were not slander because they aimed at the system and not the man, Harper declared. Ridicule these pieces were, but ridicule was not the foundation of slander.

Testimony of the three witnesses Harper dismissed as indicating no personal malice. Cobbett's remarks to the three doctors may have been hasty and ill-tempered, but to call them the mark of deliberate malice was a perversion of terms. The threats to attack Rush were against the system. In fact, Harper emphasized with a sweeping motion of his arm that the testimony only supported this point. No damage had been sustained by the doctor, no slander had been made against his character.

"We have heard about the family of the plaintiff," Harper continued, "and of the keen feelings of his respectable wife, of which not a doubt can be entertained. I should never have thought it my duty to hazard my respectability by standing here to advocate a man who should slander Dr. Rush or his very respectable wife or family. Far be it from me. I should rather have consigned him and his cause to the fate they would deserve. My professional name should never have borne the blot such conduct would justly attach to it. But this I conceive not to be the case. That my client has overstepped the bounds of good manners and decorum I have admitted, but that he had a right to run down what he believed to be a mischievous system, I have contended for and still wish to impress upon your minds. His conduct must meet with strong disapprobation, but agreeable to the rules of law and justice he merits your verdict. Neither a breach of good nanners nor harsh opprobious epithets can be construed to mean *slander*."

## 24 *"The Nature of Man Aspires After Truth"*

THE trial lasted through two days. As it proceeded, charges and countercharges between the lawyers grew sharper and more acrimonious. A feeling of tension kept increasing, a suspense shared by the spectators and even the people waiting out in the hall and on the street.

How the current seemed to be running, for or against whom, was hard to guess. However, people's sympathies appeared to favor Dr. Rush. Perhaps the Philadelphians resented Cobbett's absence in New York, or perhaps his lawyers were not building a case strong enough to counteract the emphatic charges of the prosecution. Several times minor demonstrations occurred in the courtroom, to none of which the justices seemed to pay any attention whatever.

The news would not reach Philadelphia for several days, but on the Saturday morning of the trial's second day General George Washington lay seriously ill at Mount Vernon of a septic sore throat. At the hour the trial resumed, three doctors were in consultation on the general's case. One of them was Dr. Elisha Dick, who happened to have been at one time a pupil of Benjamin Rush—the only one of the three doctors to study under the Philadelphia physician.

The decision by majority vote of the doctors was to continue bleeding the general. In all, he was bled four times during that day. Paradoxically, Dr. Dick expressed the one dissenting opinion on the quantity of bleeding. He thought at one point that bleeding had been sufficient and should be discontinued. The contrary opinions of the other two physicians outweighed his.

By ten o'clock that night General Washington would be lying dead, to the intense grief of the entire nation. Certain posthumous conjectures were to arise that his death was actually caused by excessive bleeding, not by the throat condition at all. Inevitably, and for years afterward, the name of Dr. Benjamin Rush was to be connected with the blame.

178

The second day of the trial distinguished itself for flights of oratory, arguments, and wrangling, additional pieces of evidence including more clippings from *Porcupine's Gazette* on one side and in rebuttal additional letters written by Dr. Rush. Justice Shippen took a hand in some of the disputes regarding legal meanings of words, but otherwise the judges sat as stoically as the jurors themselves.

The man who underscored the essence of the case and flung it before the jury as a historical milestone was Rush's lawyer, Moses Levy.

He came before the judges and the jury softly, almost deferentially. Clad in his robes he appeared older than his thirty-two years. His face was rather long and his nose hooked. Yet Levy's expression was softened by his dark eyes, bright and alert, gentle, somewhat sad. He was said to be the first Jewish lawyer of the Philadelphia bar, to which he was admitted at the age of twenty-three.

This was not legally a special action for slander, he told the jury in opening his address. Its nature was an action for a libel. An action for slander and an action for libel were differently understood in courts of justice.

"Words may irritate and rankle. They may even blast the character of a man upon whom they are spoken, but they perish the moment they pass out of the mouth of the speaker, and the shortness of their duration lessens their importance. But what is committed to paper—what is *printed*—has a lasting impression and is capable of much and universal mischief. It exists through the ages. It is not confined to the seat of its birth, but may extend even to the remotest parts of the earth. There can be no bounds to its effects. For words, however public, the law has provided no punishment. The law does not consider the public peace so far injured thereby as to command the public officer to issue protection. But words committed to paper demand more attention because their effects are more extensive. Taking notice, therefore, as the law does by this point of distinction between words spoken and slander committed through the press, the offense is defined."

Under the old definition of law, he explained, slander was by spoken word, libel by printed word.

Yet, Levy pointed out, the law provided certain restrictions even for the spoken word. Words hurting a man's trade or livelihood, such as calling a tradesman a bankrupt, a lawyer a knave, or a *physician a quack,* were good grounds for action unless the defendant proved no malice to be intended. The burden thus was put on the defendant.

He said of this case, "The law is pointedly against the defendant, he having written what would have been a libel even if spoken. I shall take it for granted then that this newspaper attacking Dr. Rush as *'quack,' 'potent quack,' 'grand empyric,' 'who has slain his tens of thousands,'* is a gross and infamous libel, except it should be made to appear otherwise by extenuating and giving it a mild aspect.

"All of you follow some business, and you cannot be ignorant of the violence and effects of an attack on the means you use to execute that business. You who are merchants must conceive of the danger a newspaper publication declaring you a bankrupt would be to you. It would wound your reputation so as to effectuate your ruin by stopping your credit and your trade. It would be no excuse to your opponent to say it was but a jest. Picture to yourselves, if you can, how you would feel if situated as is the plaintiff! Of what avail would it be to you to be told that it was only *ridicule?* Suppose an infamous picture was put before your door—suppose a pair of horns, describing the conduct of your wife, and that repeatedly, would you be satisfied at being told it was 'a test of truth'
180

and that 'ridicule could do you no injury'? Suppose it was a label put that you were guilty of this or that species of swindling, or worse, suppose this to be inserted in the newspaper—suppose that instead of low, indecent vulgarity you were attacked with keen satire—would it be to your benefit that you were cut with a *sharp* knife?"

The jury could not help but listen to this appeal. Levy's eloquence impressed the crowded courtroom. He went on to describe Cobbett's attacks on the doctor during the yellow-fever epidemic, and people leaned forward to catch every word. Cobbett had presumed to degrade the most respectable men of the country. Dr. Rush's sentiments were "too republican," Cobbett had said. He attacked the doctor as a physician because he resented his political views! Levy warmed to his cause.

Then he delivered one of the timeless arguments rising from the case: "The press is of incalculable benefit. It is the great road to information. The nature of man is formed to aspire after truth, but it must come into the minds of men by a series of steps, one leading to another. The press is a very important help in this progress, because by it we discover in one part of the world what has transpired at the most distant part of it. Thus improvements in arts and science are made. It is for its inestimable general use we value it. Do we value it because it furnishes any man who is able to purchase a set of type and paper with means to blacken another man's character?

"It is necessary to encourage the press, but shall it be done at the hazard of character—of all that is dear to man, his very means of sustenance? If so, instead of increasing our knowledge and happiness, it would operate as the greatest curse upon frail humanity. There is no principle in government, in philosophy, or in religion, that is so sacred but the fangs of envy might successfully attack it through the licentious use of the press. But if

181

the aim of an individual is to improve the sciences for the happiness of man in any way, he ought to be protected and encouraged. If his reasoning is fair and candid, if his arguments are addressed to the understanding, if he shows a design of increasing the mass of knowledge among mankind—to him the press ought to be free. By this means man is wrested from ignorance and made as near to angelic as his nature will admit.

"The opinions of Dr. Rush were circulated from an idea that they were just," the lawyer cried, his eyes blazing now. "He submitted them to public search and inquiry. We do not contend that Dr. Rush has established the true mode of practice; he thinks so, and has given the world his reasons for thinking so. But the case does not rest upon that point, it is all one to you whether his practice is right or wrong. Did Cobbett say that he knew a better mode? No. He endeavored to raise a public laugh upon Dr. Rush, and put him forth in a most degrading point of view at a moment when the state of the city was enough to appall the strongest heart, when the confidence of men in general was placed on the advice of this man. At that moment his reputation is pulled down. His method of treatment, almost the only one then practiced, is destroyed and no effort is made to put another in its place!

"Dr. Rush does not pretend to say he is right. He thinks so. But the superior genius of Cobbett does presume to declare that Dr. Rush is wrong, and that he has killed his tens of thousands."

Moses Levy paused. Staring at each one of the jury, he said, "The true system is not discovered perhaps, or ever may be. It might be like the dreadful earthquake that desolates the world, no means ever found to arrest its awful progress. It lies behind a veil through which the human sight cannot penetrate. But our duty and our interest require that, though we may never find the cause
182

and cure, we should be indefatigable in our endeavors to do it. Perhaps we shall only find the method of avoiding, by keeping out of its way. But, I ask, is it probable we shall ever be able to discover any means of prevention or cure if an individual shall be allowed to vent his malice at a period so momentous? Allow that with impunity, and no efforts will ever in future be made to appall this foul destroyer, no man will fortify himself for that kind of attack." Levy moved away from the jury and turned to look over the crowded courtroom. He said, "Who knows but this scandal might have prevented thousands from applying to Dr. Rush for advice? We see the defendant stand upon the high ground of boasting of his income from the number of persons who bought and read his papers. We may thence conclude that this slander extended very wide, and therefore to attempt at forming an estimate of special damages would be fruitless. To prove this negative would be impossible, and therefore cannot be expected from us. Who would come to Dr. Rush and say, 'I should have employed you had I not read such a character of you. You have murdered thousands, and therefore I could not trust my life to you.' To estimate damages, gentlemen, must be your province.

"Gentlemen, the question of damages often came before the courts in England, of which we have some accounts in the books. They are not always guided by pecuniary circumstances, but more to enforce the law and show example. The law has there estimated the fine for seducing a man's wife at ten thousand pounds sterling. Here is no pecuniary injury sustained, but a very heavy fine laid. Often it may happen that a man has a bad wife, and her loss is a real profit to him, but this is not the measure of the fine. Though less than that sum is usually laid, yet it is always exemplary.

"We find other cases mentioned in the books. A

183

journeyman printer was illegally seized for one of his publications. He was detained but six hours in custody, and during that time treated with beefsteaks and beer. On examining this in a court, the jury gave three hundred pounds sterling damages. The fact was not the pecuniary injury sustained by the man but the political consequences. In another case four thousand pounds damages was laid for a reflection on the chastity of a lady. These, gentlemen, are instances of exemplary damages, and that is what we ask for in the present case by your verdict.

"Dr. Rush has a wife and children arrived at ages capable of reading newspapers. Can any man sit by with patience when he sees his children cry, or his wife in tears in consequence of the perpetual newspaper abuse lavished upon a tender husband and a loving father? Abuse and reproach the most heart-rending, no less than a murderer and a quack. Suppose yourselves for a moment in his situation, and say whether the measure of this newspaper libeling ought to be confined merely to the damages any individual could sustain from it, or whether it ought not to be made a public example on account of the principle.

"It is high time to rescue the American character from the indifference which has too long prevailed among us. It is time to punish crime so daring. This man has declared that he would 'persecute the plaintiff while living and his memory after his death.' How can you check this vindictive spirit but by timely and exemplary punishment? Let him be taught that he has wantonly attacked, and with cool, deliberate malice, an unoffending individual. Though he has removed himself out of the jurisdiction of this court, let him know that he is a marked man, and that a respectable jury of Philadelphia have studied only principles of truth and justice with impartiality. Let others be taught by his punishment to avoid his offense."

184

THE case went on, Edward Tilghman arguing next for
Cobbett. The jurors listened patiently, and Justice Shippen
continued to make notes. But Levy's speech had impressed
the crowd. Their sympathies were turning more obviously
to Rush. The feeling was contagious, as an electric current might pass from one to another sitting so close together. The ridicule heaped by Peter Porcupine on the
head of their sacrificing doctor no longer seemed in its
courtroom repetition very funny. Somewhere injustice had
been done. All Philadelphians had a share in it.

So Tilghman's audience was not receptive as he made
points for the defendant. The lawyer sensed it. "William
Cobbett, my client, though an alien, is entitled to all the
advantages which law and justice can bestow!" he cried.
He accused Rush's counsel of being overzealous and unfair.
But Tilghman's manner was rough, and he had a naturally
unpleasant voice as he addressed the jury:

"May we not suppose, after all this, that Mr. Cobbett
is a man more sinned against then sinning? I must say he
is not without some merit. Whatever his motive, he certainly did at a critical period give a very seasonable and
proper alarm to this country, an alarm which did much
toward uniting our citizens to preserve the honor of our
country and which tended much to rescue us from European influences and attachments. Twice bills of indictment against him were sent to grand juries, and both were
returned *ignoramus*. All this is foreign to the question at
present, but the plaintiff's counsel having departed to
derogate, we may be allowed to *extenuate*."

He carried this line further, turning the attack against
the doctor. "The fever of 1793 you well remember. Dr.

185

Rush stayed in the city, no doubt from a sense of duty. But it cannot be supposed that he had no sense of the profit. He expected to be paid for his labor—"

Someone among the crowd hissed. Tilghman could feel an undercurrent grumble of protest. He plunged on hastily. "Notwithstanding that, his exertions did him very great honor. I do not pretend to justify such an attack on the system he practiced, but I do not think that condemning the system was libelous. I am sure that when the doctor came to take even seventy or eighty ounces of blood he was under the most perfect conviction that it was necessary to save the life of his patient, and that in all his practice he was actuated by the most honest motives. Inquisitive minds, like that of Dr. Rush, are not of a cast to boggle at adopting strong measures, especially when convinced of their utility. To us it was new. The use of mercurial purges and bleeding to so vast an amount was entirely unheard of by us. Therefore it was no wonder that the practice should spread an alarm of nearly as serious a nature as the fever itself.

"Dr. Rush was so confident of the success of his system that in a letter addressed to his fellow citizens on the twelfth of September, 1793, he assures them 'there is no more danger from it—the fever—when these remedies have been used in the early stage, than there is from the measles or influenza.' But with all his success, and though he stood *foremost and nearly alone,* as his counsel say, there was a destruction in that year of nearly five thousand persons. Stories of bleeding and purging were much exaggerated in the relation, so as to harass the public mind extremely. Indeed, the physicians themselves were much divided. One set of doctors contended this was the true mode, and the other another. In this state of uncertainty and indecision things remained until the fever again un-
186

happily broke out in 1797, and with it the doctors' quarrels. Not even the respectable learned institutions were exempt, the College of Physicians and the Medical Academy. I believe the difference between these bodies still exists—"

Tilghman was interrupted here by Rush's counsel. It was pointed out to the jury that the differences in the medical profession at the present time were confined to the origin of the fever. The College of Physicians at this point had agreed with Dr. Rush's system for the treatment of yellow fever.

Tilghman went on to discuss the charge of murder, saying that no one could suppose that the defendant meant the charge seriously. Cobbett used the only weapon he possessed—ridicule. "In this sense 'ridicule is surely the test of truth,'" Tilghman said, "however the ingenuous gentleman may have used it. If the defendant had meant that Dr. Rush went on murderously rejoicing at the direful effects of his system, it surely would have been a libel of the most egregious nature, but the idea cannot be proved even by the greatest ingenuity. That William Cobbett had a right to attack that system or any other we contend is indubitable, however small the stake he had among us or however short his intended stay, if he used no improper words in making that attack. If he exercised his abilities with a view to the public safety, he exercised them not only innocently but laudably. I submit to you that the publications include no design to render Dr. Rush, in his person, odious or to injure him in his business. He has here only attacked *mercury* and *bloodletting*."

Jared Ingersoll closed the arguments of the trial. He spoke at great length while the winter day turned into darkness. Yet the spectators in the courtroom kept in

187

their seats and the crowd outside the State House remained to pick up whatever news they could of the proceedings indoors.

The climax was coming, and this was no time for anyone to turn thoughts elsewhere. By now the whole city waited for the trial's outcome. The latest reports passed through the coffeehouses and taverns. The case seemed good for Rush, people said. Cobbett in his newspaper most likely had gone too far. A ferment against Cobbett spread through Philadelphia, and with disillusionment in Peter Porcupine political ideas and former hidebound opinions went toppling.

In the courtroom, where candles were being lit, Ingersoll talked on, his serious and dignified presentation giving way to anger:

"One of two things you must do," he cried to the jury. "You must either say that the character given by Cobbett to Dr. Rush—that he is a quack, a mountebank—is just, that he has either from ignorance or bad motives destroyed his fellow citizens and deserves to be banished not only from this city but from society; or the alternative presents itself—you must believe the suggestion is false and malicious, that his well-earned character has been wrested from him, for which the offender should pay damages. Compensatory damages they cannot be, but exemplary—such as should mark him hereafter as the most aggravated calumniator and detestable of characters, one whom neither sense of honor, of duty, or of propriety will restrain. Let the offender know that though the law has *leaden* feet, yet it has *iron* hands, that though slow in its operation, it is direful when once it catches its prey. . . .

"I ask you, gentlemen," Ingersoll roared, "where is anything to justify or palliate these publications, or whether they do not come up to the very *climax* of abuse
188

and vulgarity, more than I hope will ever appear again either in this or any other country!"

Speaking of Rush, Ingersoll said, "But even supposing he did fall into an error, shall he be held up to the world as the most remorseless of murderers? We are told by the learned counsel on the other side that 'ridicule is the test of truth.' I deny the position. It is possible, to be sure, to render *truth* a *ridicule*. In the same manner you may dress a wise man in a fool's cap. This maxim, so long ago exploded by the greater part of mankind, must now be revived—its revival is worthy of the cause of the defendant! The very Gospel of Heaven, by distorting its sense and by partial representation, may be made to appear ridiculous. But this is no test of its intrinsic merits."

And again: "What means the insinuation 'that dead men tell no tales' except that Dr. Rush delighted in destroying his fellow creatures? That they are insinuations does not deduct from the criminality. It is far worse than open attack, because it adds *meanness* to *malice*."

Ingersoll referred to Cobbett's threat against the doctor because the Rittenhouse eulogium was too republican: "I trust we are all republicans. Is there a man who hears me that does not feel indignation in his breast that an *alien* should abuse him because he is a republican? The citizen of the United States who is not a republican is a traitor! . . . Has Dr. Rush from the memorable day on which he voted for and signed the declaration of our independence till the present moment ever proved himself to be any other than a republican in the constitutional sense? . . . I do not wonder at the defendant's resentment against Dr. Rush. He is one of those who in the language of the President of the United States have *done too much, suffered too much, and succeeded too well* in our glorious struggle for liberty, ever to be forgiven."

189

Then referring to Cobbett, Ingersoll cried, "It is said that the defendant was of great use at a certain time in giving an alarm to the citizens of this country against foreign influence. I will tell you how far he went, and no farther— *He did not wish to destroy, but to change this foreign influence.* He wished to destroy it when it came from one foreign country, and place it on another. But to Americans sensible of the high destinies of their country, what is it from whom the influence comes? It ought to be wholly destroyed, come whence it may from France or from Britain!"

Further on Ingersoll clenched his fist and pounded the air. "We have heard much about this liberty of the press. I think I would not yield to any man in sincere estimation of that invaluable right. I consider it the eye of our political body, and I would much rather a speck, a small blemish should remain than that by a rash and unskillful operation the noble organ itself should receive an injury. But it is difficult to run the precise line in composing the happy medium which the Constitution has formed for the support of everything which is dear to a citizen. Private reputation and character are protected by the Constitution, the great fundamental law of this state."

As he concluded his argument under the smoking candles, Jared Ingersoll characterized slander with a voice loud enough to pound into every corner of the courtroom:

"Man need not dread a worse foe—slander stabs with a word—it is the *pestilence* walking in darkness, spreading *contagion* far and wide, which the most cautious traveler cannot avoid. *Courage* cannot defend itself against the insidious attacks. It is the heart-searching *dagger* of the dark *assassin.* It is the poisoned arrow whose wound is incurable. It is the mortal sting of the deadly adder. Not *government* or *officer* or *individual* can resist its fatal ef-
190

fect without the aid of law. *Murder* is its employment, *innocence* and *merit* its prey, and *ruin* its *sport."*

It was over. The pleadings were finished, the testimony taken. The lawyers leaned over their respective tables, the courtroom stirred, whispered, began to talk. Conjectures ran wild. Out on the street crowds collected in greater numbers.

The three justices talked together briefly.

Suddenly Justice Shippen banged his gavel loudly on the table before him. The courtroom quieted instantly.

The judge shuffled papers, looked around at the spectators, then turned to the jury. He began his charge in emphatic manner: "Gentlemen—this is an action brought by the plaintiff against the defendant for writing, printing, and publishing divers scandalous libels, to defame and vilify him. The defendant has pleaded that he is not guilty. His counsel, however, have acknowledged publication of the papers which, otherwise, it would have been incumbent on the plaintiff to prove. The question, therefore, will be whether they amount in law to defamatory libels or not."

The judge told the jury that in English libel cases the only task of the jury was to judge of the fact of publication and its truth. The Court, as judges of the law, decided whether the paper amounted to a libel or not. But in the state of Pennsylvania, under the state Constitution, the jury possessed the power of judging both of the law and fact, under the Court's direction. He explained that a libel as defined by the law was the malicious defamation, expressed either in printing, writing, or by signs or pictures tending to blacken either the memory of one who was dead or the reputation of one who was alive, or to expose him to public hatred, contempt, or ridicule. In a civil suit the damages were to be assessed by the jury.

191

"The charges laid against the defendant in the declaration," Justice Shippen continued, "are various, but they may be reduced in substance to the following—that he repeatedly calls the plaintiff a quack, an empyric; charges him with intemperate bleeding, injudiciously administering mercury in large doses in the yellow fever; puffing himself off; styling him the Samson in medicine; charging him with murdering his patients and slaying his thousands and tens of thousands.

"The counts laid in the declaration are fully proved by the publications, which are certainly libelous." The justice said the word so distinctly and carefully that every person in the room caught its impact. The crowd gasped. The judge was telling them plainly! Spontaneously, people clapped.

Justice Shippen held up his hand for quiet. "In what manner do the defendant's counsel repel these proofs?" he went on. "Not by justifying the truth of the matters charged against Dr. Rush, which on the contrary they have repeatedly acknowledged to be false, but by analyzing the several allegations in the newspapers and from thence drawing a conclusion that no intentional personal malice appears, which they say is the essence of the offense." Malice rests in the heart, the judge said, and is only to be judged by the words and actions of the party. The words themselves import malice, and in that case the proof lies on the defendant to show the innocence of his intentions. "If he has done *that* to your satisfaction, you will acquit him. But as this is chiefly founded on the allegation that the attack was meant to be made on Dr. Rush's *system* and not on the *man,* it unfortunately appears that not the least attempt is made to combat the doctor's arguments with regard to the system itself. The attack is made merely by gross scurrilous abuse of the doctor himself. Added to this, one of the witnesses proves a declaration made by
192

the defendant that if Dr. Rush had not been *the man* he should never have meddled with *the system*."

Justice Shippen leaned forward in his chair, and spoke very slowly for greatest emphasis. "Another ground of defense is of a more serious nature, as it leads to an important question on our Constitution. It is said that the subject of dispute between the plaintiff and the defendant was a matter of public concern as it related to the health and lives of our fellow citizens, and that by the words of our Constitution every man has a right to discuss such subjects in print. The liberty of the press, gentlemen, is a valuable right in every free country, and ought never to be unduly restrained. But when it is perverted to the purposes of private slander, it then becomes a most destructive engine in the hands of unprincipled men. The utmost purity and integrity of heart is no shield against the shafts and arrows of malice, conveyed to the world by printed publications. Verbal slander may be frequently very injurious, but slander in writing or print, being more generally disseminated and more durable in its effects, is consequently infinitely more pernicious and provoking. Our state Constitution of 1790 contains certainly very general words with relation to the right of a citizen to print his thoughts and offer them to the consideration of the public, but at the same time it guards against the generality of the privilege by expressly declaring that every person availing himself of the liberty of the press *should be responsible for the abuse of that liberty,* thus securing to our citizens the invaluable right of reputation against every malicious invader of it."

The room was quiet, as if everyone were holding his breath. The sudden consciousness filled the whole courtroom that this trial was indeed a test of American principles, far exceeding in meaning the personal conflict of two men.

The law considered published attacks on private character as an atrocious offense, the judge said. They threatened public peace. If courts provided no redress, men naturally would take satisfaction in their own way, leading to duels, murders, and perhaps assassinations.

He told the jury that their principal consideration would be the damages they were to assess. In this respect they were the almost uncontrollable judges. It was their province. "The Court have indeed the power to order a new trial where damages are excessive," Justice Shippen explained, "but in cases of torts and injuries of this kind the lawbooks say the damages must be so outrageously disproportionate to the offense as at first blush to shock every person who hears of it before the Court will order a new trial."

A moment passed before the people fully comprehended the extent of what he had said. Even the jurors themselves appeared startled. One or two of them smiled a little. Then a burst of applause shook the room. Hearing it, the crowd outside began to cheer. Had Rush won already? they wanted to know.

The judge held up his hand again, and finished his charge rapidly. "Everyone must know that offenses of this kind have for some time past too much abounded in our city. It seems high time to restrain them. That task is with you, gentlemen. To suppress so great an evil, it will not only be proper to give compensatory, but exemplary, damages, thus stopping the growing progress of this daring crime. At the same time," he cautioned, "the damages should not be so enormous as absolutely to ruin the offender."

One more final sentence was spoken rapidly, but no one listened anyway—that no party considerations should ever have place in this court, and the gentlemen were entreated to banish them entirely from their breasts. . . .

194

Dr. Rush took Julia home after that, leaving their son Richard to wait for the verdict. They had trouble pushing through the crowd surrounding the State House with so many people holding out hands of congratulations to the doctor and his wife as if he had already won. Well, hadn't the judge's instructions been clear enough to determine the verdict? Practically so. Yet as they escaped from the mass of eager Philadelphians and drove home through the night, the doctor felt cold with apprehension. The road had been too long to believe now they had come to the end.

The jury returned to the courtroom after two hours. The judges came back, and by now the spectators were packed in to the last inch of space.

*The verdict of the jury was in favor of Dr. Benjamin Rush, in the sum of five thousand dollars.*

The crowded room heard and spontaneously broke into such clapping as was unprecedented and unrecorded in any Pennsylvania court. The applause was taken up outdoors by wild shouts. "Rush wins!" The news spread over the city like the tide of the sea. Benjamin Rush was the city's hero, its savior, its defender against tyrannical impostors as well as disease.

The friends of William Cobbett were stunned. *Five thousand dollars!* The amount was appalling, unheard of. So this was republican justice. Silently they left the courtroom, those who had attended the trial. Among them went Benjamin North, Porcupine's faithful friend.

Federalists everywhere soon heard the decision, those arch-Federalists who retained Tory ways of thinking. Then they could see the handwriting on the wall as Cobbett himself had already seen it. Liberty in America was to have a more universal meaning for all its citizens than

195

they had ever dreamed. Politics had, after all, become a part of the trial. According to the jury's verdict, the concept of liberty was not going to be restricted to any narrow base.

The principles expressed by Benjamin Rush in his Rittenhouse eulogium had passed their own "test of truth," and could forevermore stand free in the United States.

Richard Rush hurried home to tell his parents.

"You've won, Father. Five thousand dollars!"

Dr. Rush stared at him. Julia was the one to cry, "God's will be done!" She put her arms around her husband's shoulders.

"Yes," Benjamin Rush said. "I thank Thee, not for myself—"

He thought of future thousands, perhaps millions, of sick persons who would recover from disease under medical knowledge free to expand without prejudiced restraint.

*Verdict Sustained*

# 26

## *Monday in New York*

I N the city of New York on the late afternoon of Monday, December 17, a sharp, chill wind blew between the rivers. Darkness came early out of winter's grayness. William Cobbett turned his collar up as he strode through the streets toward the temporary boarding-house where he stayed with his wife and two children. All day he had tramped through the town looking for a place to rent which would be suitable for a combined bookshop and dwelling. Among those he had seen, one on Water Street caught his fancy. He would take Nancy to look at it.

To find a suitable house was not easy considering the rent he could afford now. Moving from Philadelphia to New York, combined with the suspension of his publications, meant considerable financial loss. So his resources would not permit any extravagance at all until he could re-establish a bookselling business. For the moment he had no plans for resuming any newspaper or periodical publication, except for one last "farewell" issue of *Porcupine's Gazette*.

199

His broad shoulders hunched forward against the wind, Cobbett appeared massive in his heavy coat and wide-brimmed hat. Some people turned to look and wonder at the unfamiliar figure walking with such purpose. New Yorkers knew him by name if not by sight, except for those few such as Alexander Hamilton, who had made a special point of meeting him in Philadelphia.

By the time he reached the half-timbered lodging-house twilight hung low and seemed to swirl over rooftops with the breeze. He came to the door and reached for a key in his pocket.

Another figure moved out of the shadows to greet him. "Mr. Cobbett—"

"Eh? Who is it? Ben North! What are you doing here, from Philadelphia?"

"I waited outside, hearing from Mrs. Cobbett you'd be home shortly enough. 'Tis almighty cold out here, I can vouch for that. I thought it best to tell you here 'stead o' indoors where—well, she might hear."

"*She* might hear? For God's sake, man, what is it? What's happened?"

Benjamin North glanced up worriedly. He had come as quickly as he could, he said. If Mr. Cobbett had not heard it yet—the trial had gone against him.

"Against me?" Cobbett drew a deep breath. "I'm not too surprised at that." Suddenly he clutched North's lapel. "You're not saying everything. What more?"

"It's the damages—that jury—"

"How much?"

"Five thousand dollars, Mr. Cobbett."

"*Five*—" Even in the dim light North saw purple shadows rising in his friend's face. Cobbett choked. He turned away and walked off a few steps, then came back. "Tell me exactly what happened."

"You ought to have heard the judge, he didn't leave you a chance. The lawyers—" North shook his head.
200

Cobbett's teeth gritted as he made a snarling sound in his throat. "Dirty democrats! That bloodstained doctor sat there and heard all this, I expect? He thinks to collect *five thousand dollars* from me?"

"His son, the lawyer one, has already come to New York to get execution of the judgment."

For just one instant Cobbett might have sagged. His shoulders gave and his head bowed. But instantly he straightened up.

"Come in out of the cold," he said. He reached for the front doorknob, then paused. "Before we go in to Mrs. Cobbett, I might as well assure you now that I am not cast down for one moment. I'll *never* be cast down by that infamous herd of Philadelphians!"

"Mr. Tilghman has written to you," North said hurriedly. "He advises you to get out of the country before the writ for the judgment is served on you—"

Cobbett rose on his toes, a mighty shadow of wrath in the darkness. "Mr. North!" he roared, "though I may be robbed of the money, my *honor* will never be sold for five thousand dollars! I am an Englishman. To run away would be disgraceful and cowardly! I've preserved my reputation so far, and I won't tarnish it for my children."

"Yes—I mean—no," North answered.

"Never mind," Cobbett said, pointing a finger at North. "While I have my soul they can't ruin me. I think I've plans already to even this score. I may have to retreat, Mr. North, but if I do I promise *I'll fight to the very water's edge!* Let's go indoors. . . ."

## 27   And Monday in Philadelphia

ON THAT same Monday afternoon, in Philadelphia, Dr. Rush's carriage rolled through the gates of the Pennsylvania Hospital on Eighth Street at Pine. The old guardian doffed his hat. He had known the doctor these many years, and he had the highest respect for him. He had never believed the stories circulating among the staff in the building. Hadn't Dr. Rush cured his own daughter of pulmonary consumption by more than twenty bleedings after most of the physicians of the city gave her up as incurable? Let others speak as they would.

Farther on, Peter Place, the hospital gardener, waved a response to the doctor's greeting. At this time of year he had little to do. The fallen leaves from the buttonwood trees in the yard had long since been burned. He came forward to take the doctor's horse.

"A fine afternoon, sir," he said.

"It is, Mr. Place. Cold enough but not too sharp."

The Pennsylvania Hospital was a three-story building surrounded by a yard a full square's width and depth. The high enclosing wall gave it a permanent feeling of isolation from the rest of the city, a comfortable impression of its being a world of its own. When first built, the hospital had been out in the country remote from the odors and stagnant refuse common to the town, but at this time the streets had been extended through farmland, and the city's fringes closed around. The entrance through the old east wing had been completed more than forty years before, long prior to the Revolution. To the left of the entrance door was the cornerstone with an inscription written especially by Dr. Benjamin Franklin.

Rush walked up the steps, feeling under his shoes the familiar indentations worn into the marble by the feet which had ascended here.

In the hospital's front hallway a handwritten notice had been affixed to a nail on the wall. The doctor paused to glance at it:

Pennsylvania Hospital: The sitting managers of the Pennsylvania Hospital for this month are: Law-

rence Seckel, merchant, 155 High Street, Israel Pleas-
ants, merchant, 74 South Second Street. The attending
physicians for this month are: Benjamin Rush, M.D.,
corner of Fourth and Walnut Streets, Philip Syng
Physick, M.D., 45 Arch Street. Applications for admission must be in the first instant to either of these two
physicians. . . . Recent fractures, if taken immediately as they happen, will be received at the gate as
usual without waiting for the form of admission. Published by order of the Board of Managers, Samuel
Coates, Secretary.

Rush continued on up the stairway to the women's
ward. Miss Prudence Mercer, one of the hospital nurses,
joined him there almost at once. Few patients were in the
ward, and Dr. Rush moved rapidly from bed to bed without the necessity of delaying long for details. He spoke to
one woman admitted for sore legs, and instructed the
nurse to continue salve applications.

Another patient, one Catherine Brennon, in the hospital for dropsy, had improved steadily after bleeding and
salivation. Rush examined her briefly.

"Madam, I think you are sufficiently cured to go
home," he told her. "Miss Mercer, you may see that she is
discharged today."

"Yes, sir." The nurse smiled. To her Benjamin Rush
was the greatest doctor in the world. She had watched him
work many times, and knew his sureness of touch, his
careful deliberation, his skillful bedside diagnosis. She
heard so often expressions of praise and virtual adoration
from his students. It was wonderful he had won the case
against the wicked Peter Porcupine.

At the far end of the ward a woman lay in bed tim-
idly watching his approach. As he came up to her she
looked away.

"Well, Mary," Dr. Rush said. "I'm glad to see you
have taken my advice. You will be cared for kindly here."

The case record named her as Mary Beatty, with

203

syphilis, poor list, Joseph Budd and John Ormroyd securities for her clothing and burial expenses if she died. Hospital rules required each patient on the poor list to have a securities pledge for the sum of five dollars to defray possible interment expenses.

"We have already applied mercury on the sores of affected areas," Miss Mercer said.

Dr. Rush nodded. "Also give mercury for salivation," he ordered. He spoke to the patient again. "You will do as the nurse tells you? It will be necessary to excite the saliva in your mouth to a great degree, possibly to the loss of a full pint. You will understand the discomfort is for your own cure?"

The woman nodded, glanced at the nurse. But Miss Mercer was following Dr. Rush from the ward. . . .

Shortly afterward the doctor crossed rapidly from the hospital's east wing to the separate west wing. The central portion of the hospital was still under construction. Work proceeded slowly for lack of funds. As he moved around piles of brick and lumber, Dr. Rush glanced up into the building's framework. The section would complete the hospital's facilities, providing an operating amphitheater with surrounding benches for students' use, more space for beds, even a library.

Benjamin Rush's special interest was the west wing. Here was the madhouse, finished three years before.

If he had chosen, though it was not his usual nature to speak of his work for others, Rush could have taken credit for the existence of the madhouse. He had been first to see the necessity for such a building. He had persuaded the board of managers to construct it, and through newspaper writings he had stirred the people of the city into realizing the desperate need for proper facilities to care for persons afflicted with mental illness. Formerly maniacs had been placed in dark cells in the east-wing basement. There had been a time when Philadelphians made Sunday-afternoon picnic excursions to the hospital grounds bringing long sticks to poke through the barred windows, baiting the mad ones into frenzy. This kind of holiday entertainment became so popular that to discourage it the managers fixed an admission fee to the grounds.

For the past twelve years Benjamin Rush had been the physician in charge of the hospital's mentally deranged. He had brought about not only improvements in care, but an increasing recognition that madness was a form of physical as well as mental illness. Now patients had a certain privacy, fresh air and light, more adequate nursing. Rush had obtained connecting bathrooms on the first floor of the west wing for the hot and cold bath treatments. He arranged special manual work programs for patients capable of performing them. Instead of following the prevailing feeling toward maniacs as hopeless curiosities, the hospital had finally been persuaded to treat them with more gentle understanding and hope for at least some proportion of cure.

Two student apprentices joined the doctor. They stopped at the cell of a young woman whose case had been particularly disappointing. A month ago she had been so much relieved of her madness that she had been discharged to go home. One week later she was back at the hospital. Dr. Rush found her today standing in the center of her small room, chained to the floor. On seeing him she burst into tears, moaning pitifully. Once the girl must have been pretty, but now her hair was unkempt and her clothing torn. The room with windows closed against the winter cold was filled with the sour stench from the chamber pot under the straw-covered bed.

Dr. Rush kept control of his temper. He turned to

205

the students. "I've told you cleanliness is prerequisite to cure. This room is not clean. Have you been following the treatment prescribed?"

"Yes, sir," one replied quickly. "Hot and cold baths, and she's been bled ten ounces today, as every day. I'm sorry, sir—"

"Continue until there is improvement, or until I order otherwise," the doctor snapped. "Has she been purged?"

"Calomel and jalap yesterday."

"Please repeat tomorrow." Dr. Rush reached out to take the girl's elbow. He drew her arm down gently from her face. The moaning stopped. He said to her, "Hannah, you have not been doing your sewing lately. You remember the handkerchief you were to make for me? Perhaps soon, Hannah, do you think?"

She looked at him with reddened eyes. Slowly she nodded.

"I have every hope for her yet," Dr. Rush said as they left the room. "I believe the bleeding and baths will effect at least relief."

The remainder of the cases were routine. Some were patients of apparently incurable derangement, but others among the men were cheerfully doing carpenter work or grinding Indian corn in a handmill to feed the hospital's horse and milk cows. A few of the women patients were sewing in quite normal manner.

The doctor was ready to leave. One of the students coughed shyly. "We're glad about the trial, Dr. Rush," he said.

"I guess everybody is," the other added.

It had grown dark when the doctor walked down the hospital steps. He made his way to the carriage. His step was lighter than for many months. The clouds had lifted at last, he believed on that evening. . . .

## 28 *"You Are a Father, Too!"*

IN JANUARY the New York stage brought to Philadelphia copies of William Cobbett's farewell issue of *Porcupine's Gazette*. The paper devoted itself to a summary of the results of the trial. In typical Cobbett manner, the *Gazette* took special care to point out that General Washington had died on the same day the jury rendered its verdict. Washington died of the effects of Dr. Rush's bloodletting and purging system—at least, Porcupine said so. It was conclusive evidence, he claimed, of the deadly results of the doctor's teaching.

Years would pass before the taint of that insinuation disappeared from Rush's reputation.

But the *Gazette* was merely the beginning, a promise of the ferocity of William Cobbett's revenge.

Shortly after the middle of February, when Philadelphians might be supposed to have forgotten the trial, a new publication arrived in the city. A number of copies were furnished to one of the local bookstores, and as word went around the copies were sold almost overnight. In the briefest time nearly everyone in Philadelphia was reading William Cobbett's latest.

What he had published was one of the most devastating, vicious printed attacks ever let loose against one man. In it he blasted Benjamin Rush with a scorn and venom that made pale by comparison anything Cobbett had previously written about anyone. It was a battery of savage retaliatory fury.

He called his paper the *Rushlight*. This was the first

number, and he promised more to come. He was not actuated by revenge, he announced, but only by a sense of duty in holding up in their true light the Rushes, the Hopkinsons, the Meases, and the rest of the tribe. He promised to expose the conduct of Rush, the witnesses, the lawyers, judges, and even the jury concerned in the trial he had lost. Such exposure was demanded in justice to the people of America, foreign nations, and particularly in justice to Englishmen who might be deceived by false ideas of American liberty. He agreed to furnish a full narrative of those judicial proceedings which had dealt so severely with him merely on account of his being, he was convinced, a British subject.

The first issue of the *Rushlight* discussed Dr. Rush—thirty-eight pages' worth—with a five-page addendum on Dr. Mease, Rush's witness. "Can the *RUSH* grow up without mire?" Cobbett quoted from the Book of Job. The rush withers before any other herb, he pointed out. If Rush's lawyers had confined themselves to the only subject that ought to have been submitted to the jury, had they not gone out of their way to extol the *family* and *character*—"had they not held him up as an 'Hippocrates' and a 'saving angel,' while they represented me as a 'wretch cast up from the very dregs and slime of the community, that ought to have rotted in obscurity'; had they not thus insolently, and I may add foolishly, provoked an inquiry—" then, Cobbett said, the family and character of Rush would have remained with him objects of as perfect insignificance as the poverty-bred plant, the name of which he bore, and the worthlessness of which was proverbial.

He described the doctor's character. "Rush is remarkable for insinuating manners and for that smoothness and softness of tongue which the mock quality call *politeness,* but which the profane vulgar call *blarney.* To see and hear him, you would think he was all friendship and humanity. He shakes hands with all he meets; everyone is his *dear friend,* all the people his *dear fellow citizens,* and all the creation his *dear fellow creatures.* . . . If making fair weather with men of all religions and all parties be a proof of merit, I know of no person so meritorious as Rush."

Cobbett attacked Rush's intolerance, his insolent pretension to superiority, his writing—"most disgusting egotism that ever soiled paper." In passing mention he referred to Joseph Hopkinson as "my dear little Hail Columbia," explaining in a footnote that Hopkinson had written a wretched song with that title.

But nothing could hurt Benjamin Rush as much as Cobbett's scathing remarks on his family.

He described how Hopkinson toward the close of a dozen pages of lies, nonsense, and bombast during the trial had given the tender-hearted jury a piteous picture of the distress in Rush's family by his publications against their "immaculate father." No Philadelphian could be duped by this miserable rant, Cobbett said.

He went on to recount an episode that actually had occurred during the summer epidemic of 1797. A Dr. Andrew Ross in Philadelphia had been suspected of being the anonymous author of a violent newspaper article against Rush. It turned out that the article was actually written by Dr. Currie, but meantime Rush's oldest son John had accused Ross. The resulting tangle brought a challenge from the headstrong John to Dr. Ross for calling him an impudent puppy, a street fight between them, and a challenge from Ross to Benjamin Rush himself for instigating his son's violence. Rush would not be drawn into a duel. "I do not fear death," he replied to Ross, "but I dare not offend God by exposing myself or a fellow creature to the chance of committing murder." It had been an unfortunate episode during the high-strung days of

Cobbett's original newspaper attacks. By now, almost three years later, the Rush family wished to forget the incident. But Cobbett gleefully described every detail, repeating the epithet of "impudent puppy" against John, and calling the whole matter "the most vindictive, the most base, the most foul, and dastardly act that ever was committed in the face of day."

The effect of the *Rushlight* was catastrophic. Overnight the benefit of the lawsuit victory was washed out. Rush realized how Philadelphians relished a scandalous paper. The supply in the shops was quickly exhausted, and copies were loaned from hand to hand all over the city. His children at school faced jeering remarks, and on the streets they were shouted at: *"How is old Hipprocrates, purge 'em, boys!"*

When John Rush read that first issue, he turned pale. He noted the references to his father, the rest of the family, and to himself. He was twenty-three at this time, a highly emotional young man who seemed to have inherited his father's impetuousness without the steadying balance of temperament. He was a lieutenant in the medical department of the new United States Navy, at home on leave after serving in the undeclared sea war against the French.

John went upstairs and packed his clothes. He did not even stop to change from his navy undress uniform. He left the house and caught the mail stage for New York. His father was out on calls. No one else could stop him.

Benjamin Rush returned home that day in melancholy mood. Everywhere he heard the same thing: *You've seen William Cobbett's latest? It's a shame, Doctor, a positive shame the way he sets on you. . . .*

A shame! But the hypocrites who said it still laughed. Rush felt he would go out of his mind if this thing were not stopped. Julia's distress tormented him. He worried about what his sons might yet do. Even on the news that Cobbett had started his abuse again, John had threatened to challenge him to a duel.

Rush entered the house, and Julia met him frantically, "Ben, Ben, an awful thing has happened! John— has gone to New York—"

She could not finish for the catch in her voice. Rush saw the horror in her tear-streaked face. "New York?" he gasped apprehensively.

"To see William Cobbett. I looked in his room, and he's packed his things. You know how resentful he is. Oh, Ben, I'm afraid!"

A chill ran down Rush's spine. "Don't worry," he said as gently as he could. "I'll do something at once."

It was all very well to reassure Julia. He did indeed know John's determination. His own hand shook. He went straight into his study and sat down to piece out a letter to Brockholst Livingstone, his friend and lawyer in New York.

To compose the letter was difficult. He tried it, gave up, tried again. On the paper he put down words, crossed them off. *This day my eldest son, John Rush, set off in the mail stage to attack*—he changed the last word to—*obtain satisfaction of Cobbett for the falsehoods he has published against him. His spirit is uncommonly firm and determined, and his resentments are keen upon the present occasion. I tremble therefore for the consequences of a meeting between them. The design of this letter is to call upon you as a friend to find him out and by persuasion or the force of law to arrest him in his present undertaking.* Probably Livingstone would find him near Cobbett's door. He would recognize John in his sailor's uniform.

Couldn't Cobbett be sued in New York, Rush continued—either criminally or civilly, to stop these publications? If he did continue, then he could be jailed for contempt of court. Surely New York judges would be sympathetic to a gray-headed and inoffensive citizen of Pennsylvania who heard every hour of his life murder connected with the names of his sons.

Then Rush broke down. He stopped writing and held his head in his hands. A dry, hard sob shook him. "Please, God, may I have strength. Preserve my son John—"

He picked up the pen. *You are a father,* he wrote in conclusion to Brockholst Livingstone. *Feel and act as you would wish me to do for your children in a similar situation. If assistance be necessary in conducting this business, call upon Colonel Burr or any other of your eminent lawyers. Your services shall be liberally compensated. . . .*

## 29   *The Fantastic Phenomenon from England*

AT HIS new residence on Water Street, No. 141, William Cobbett was intensely preoccupied. The second edition of the *Rushlight* was in process of composition. In it he castigated Dr. Rush's medical system with every sharp comment, instance, and barb of logic he could command. Cobbett had done considerable research for this task. All the records and files from the yellow-fever epidemic in 1793 were on his desk, and he made full use of them.

Statistics gave the number of deaths day by day. Cobbett started a list beginning with the time Rush announced discovery of his new healing system. Through the raging epidemic from mid-September to mid-October the daily death rate had climbed.

"Thus you see," Cobbett wrote swiftly, "that though the fever was on the twelfth of September reduced to a

212

level with a common cold, though the lancet was continually unsheathed, though Rush and his subalterns were ready at every call, the deaths did actually increase; and, incredible as it may seem, this increase grew with that of the very practice which saved more than 99 patients out of 100! Astonishing obstinacy! Perverse Philadelphians! Notwithstanding that precious purges were advertised at every corner and were brought even to your doors and bedsides by *old women* and *Negroes,* notwithstanding life was offered you on terms the most reasonable and accommodating, still you persisted in dying! Nor did barely dying content you. It was not enough for you to reject the means of prolonging your existence, but you must begin to drop off the faster from the moment that those means were presented to you; and this for no earthly purpose that I can see but the malicious one of injuring the reputation of the 'saving Angel' whom 'a kind Providence had sent to your assistance'!"

Cobbett wrote savagely under the sting of his lawsuit defeat. Every word cried for vengeance against the man responsible, and of bitter retribution against every individual concerned with the case.

Already he had in outline the third and fourth *Rushlights*. He would not rest until he had drawn his fill of satisfaction in measured blood of all who had trodden on him.

Brockholst Livingstone combed New York for Lieutenant John Rush. He found him finally in the lobby of a theater, during an evening performance. The young man was standing morosely off by himself, away from others of the crowd. The lawyer had a long talk with John, on the spot. The doctor's son was adamant, sullen. Brockholst Livingstone, in his fifties, one of the ablest and most successful lawyers in the country, was ultimately

213

destined for the United States Supreme Court. Yet all his ability and power of argument could not extract an agreement from young John to leave Cobbett alone. The best Livingstone could get was a promise to think it over. It was a disappointing report to have to send back to the boy's father in Philadelphia.

And two days later an army officer called at William Cobbett's bookshop.

"Mr. Cobbett, sir?" he said stiffly. "I am Captain Still of the artillery, Fort Jay. I have come on behalf of my friend, Lieutenant John Rush of the navy."

"Rush!" Cobbett growled. "I do not wish to hear anything of the Rushes."

The captain looked around the store. Customers were there, already glancing curiously in his direction.

"I wish a private interview with you, Mr. Cobbett," he said.

"No! The Rushes have tried to ruin me and I'll never forgive one of them! Nothing you have to say will interest me."

"Sir, my message from Lieutenant Rush is explicit—"

"Is this meant to be a challenge? If so, I refuse it!" Cobbett reached for a poker by the stove. His height and breadth grew with anger. "You may leave, sir. Tell your Rush friend he can mark me a coward whenever he wishes. Nothing he can say means anything to me. Good day!"

"You have called him a coward. May I remind you that in your paper you boasted that Lieutenant Rush had not challenged you? He is here now, sir, in my representation to you—"

"Please leave! I'll have nothing to do with this. What's more, I'll report you for this errand—"

"The lieutenant demands more satisfaction than this!"

214

"No more! Get out of here!"

By this time Mrs. Cobbett had heard the angry voices. She entered the room in time to see her husband raising the poker. But the captain did not stay. He walked out of the shop defiantly.

William Cobbett did write a letter to the Secretary of War describing the incident. Instead of mailing it, he printed it as an open letter in the *Rushlight*. John Rush took out the only revenge he could by publishing an attack of his own on Cobbett in a New York paper.

No duel took place. But tragedy nevertheless already had marked out John Rush. Within ten years he was to be an incurable maniac in his father's own wards for the mentally ill at the Pennsylvania Hospital.

The rumor reached Cobbett that Brockholst Livingstone representing Dr. Benjamin Rush was taking steps to initiate a new libel suit in New York.

When he heard this, Cobbett paced the floor thoughtfully. He had much to think about. On the one hand, his precarious financial position was improving. Sales of the *Rushlight* had been phenomenal, and the book business was good. A number of people had gratuitously come to his rescue after the Philadelphia decision and contributed to a fund toward the five-thousand-dollar fine. With his lawyers agreeing, he expected to delay payment of the damages to Dr. Rush as long as legally possible.

Meanwhile, he could take satisfaction in the devastating effect on the city of Philadelphia of his new writing. Reports from there indicated the delight with which the people were receiving the *Rushlight*. The whole Rush camp suffered with dismay, one juror threatened to sue, and Cobbett felt sure that the political prestige of Governor McKean, Judge Shippen, and the Democratic-Republicans was undermined again.

Cobbett took special pleasure in repeating the idea

to the public that the Rush medical system had been responsible for George Washington's death. He suggested as a warning to Americans that it would be a good thing if the names and addresses of all Rush's pupils were published.

There was little doubt in anyone's mind about Cobbett's writing ability, and he knew it. His old enemy Dr. Joseph Priestley, in chivalrous and certainly highly benign manner, called William Cobbett at this time by far the most popular writer in the country, and "indeed one of the best in many respects." Priestley wrote to an English friend saying that Cobbett was publishing the *Rushlight,* which in sarcastic humor was equal to if not superior to anything he had ever seen. This undoubtedly deserved tribute from one of the century's leading intellectuals added stature to the fantastic phenomenon from England.

Yet Cobbett kept thinking about the future. What was best for him to do? His campaign of retribution must inevitably run dry, grow stale in public interest. He could not exist indefinitely on a hate campaign against one man. Now the threat of a new suit arose. Another civil action might result in complete financial disaster. Or a criminal action, taken through the state, could lead to prison.

At this juncture Cobbett put on his hat and coat and went to see a good and old friend who lived in New York. . . .

Alexander Hamilton listened carefully to what William Cobbett had to say. His deep-set dark eyes hardened when his caller mentioned the name of Dr. Benjamin Rush. While Cobbett moved around the room, big and purposeful, Hamilton sat attentively in an armchair in his study.

The two men were entirely unlike in all but political

216

principles. Compared to Cobbett, Hamilton appeared small in height, more precise. His dress and manner were perfectly polished. His fair, pleasant complexion and light hair were in contrast to the younger Cobbett's physical strength. And Cobbett was angry, Hamilton thoughtful.

In basic political ideology they agreed, in that both respected the English form of government under the monarchy of George III above all other varieties. But Hamilton could compromise with the reality of American principles, while Cobbett could not. The politics of the Federalist party under Hamilton's leadership aimed to come as close as practical to a central autocratic, and aristocratic, government. Falling short of desired goals, Colonel Hamilton could accept as much less as circumstances required.

Beyond question, Alexander Hamilton owed a great debt to the English writer. For five years Cobbett's writing had supported his party, and therefore his ambitions, like a mighty bridge. But Hamilton could see what President John Adams' defection from rigid Federalist convictions made evident to anyone. Adams had rebelled, especially over the French question, and swung the balance of public opinion with him. The arch-conservative, reactionary aims of extreme Federalism were doomed in America. The outcome of the Rush trial in Philadelphia was in itself a portent. With the change in climate Cobbett himself must eventually fall, for he could never adapt his thinking to more liberal terms and remain sincere in the public eye.

Cobbett had attacked Adams for making peace with France and a number of Federalists for the sake of their own reputations were now keeping aloof from Porcupine. Hamilton was ruled by intense personal ambition. Perhaps Cobbett as a writer would still be useful as before.

But if he nourished Cobbett's support, would there be risk of an unfavorable reaction? The alternatives were in Hamilton's mind.

Dr. Rush threatened another suit, Cobbett told him. The circle tightened, and Cobbett could see it almost as plainly as Hamilton. But Hamilton hated Rush. The intense Philadelphia doctor all his life had expressed volubly that partisan spirit for democratic ideas. His annoying path kept crossing Hamilton's. There had been the episode during the Revolution of Rush's traitorous letter to Patrick Henry. As General Washington's confidential aide, Hamilton still had a memory of that affair.

". . . I could not afford remuneration equal to the value of your services," Cobbett was saying, "but if you could at least assist in the case—"

Hamilton rose from his chair. "Mr. Cobbett," he said, "if Dr. Rush brings suit in New York, I should think it an honor to defend you. I would refuse any fee at all."

Cobbett stared at him from under bushy brows.

Whether Hamilton was governed by loyalty to his once valuable supporter, or at least in part by hatred toward Rush, was known only to the colonel.

Hamilton smiled and held out his hand. "I assure you, you will not have to fear from *injustice* in New York!"

Cobbett walked home slowly from his meeting with Hamilton. The colonel had been kind to him. Nevertheless, Cobbett understood more than was said. He could not wait much longer to decide about the future, for the good of himself and his family.

Meanwhile work remained to be done. By now the third *Rushlight* was under way. He planned at least a fourth and fifth issue, and for these he intended to set the record clear with regard to Justice Shippen, Pennsyl-
218

vania's Governor McKean, and various other individuals allied with them in Pennsylvania's republican government. Let them come after him for contempt of court if they would!

For the immediate task, this third issue, William Cobbett was about to write a defense of himself. It would be a rebuttal to Rush's lawyers in the trial. *His* lawyers had failed in making their defense for him. A self-defense became even more worth while with a new suit threatening. He would defend himself so well that even the jury in Philadelphia would be shown up before the public for the rascals they were.

That was it! He would address the jury on his own behalf, in the third person, as if *he* were his own counsel. . . .

## 30 Defense in His Own Behalf

HE HURRIED home faster. The day was ending, but that did not matter. Nancy would bring him supper at his desk. She would keep the children quiet while he wrote. He formed his words in his mind:

—In making this defense I shall suppose myself in the court, and having heard the evidence and the pleadings, now replying to the whole that was urged against me. As I shall use the words, "Gentlemen of the jury," I beg leave to premise that the word "Gentlemen" will be admitted, on this occasion, for form's sake only.

—Gentlemen of the jury,

—I rise to defend a man, remarkable for his frankness, against the underhand machinations of hypocrisy. I rise to defend against a charge of slander a man who has been slandered without measure and without mercy. I rise to defend an honest, loyal, and public-spirited Briton against the false and calumnious suggestions of private malice, political prejudice, and national antipathy.

—I should degrade the character of the defendant by comparing it with that of Dr. Rush, or by submitting it to *your* investigation. To the malignant assertions of Hopkinson, Levy, and Ingersoll, I shall therefore make no reply, but shall confine myself to the subject with which alone you have, on this occasion, anything to do.

—Mr. Cobbett stands charged with having, during the prevalence of the yellow fever of 1797, published certain false and malicious slanders against Dr. Rush. The *printing* and *publishing* the defendant would rather cut off his hand than disown, but the *falsehood* and *malice* imputed to him he utterly denies. . . .

With these words William Cobbett started the self-defense published in his *Rushlight*. He worked through the evening and the following day—on and on he wrote furiously until he had enough to fill thirty-nine printed pages—an address to the jury that would have taken some hours to deliver. He poured the bitterness of his soul into that writing, yet at the same time kept it within the judicial bounds of a lawyer's brief. It is doubtful that the most learned of opposing counsel could have raised one sustainable objection to Cobbett's summing up. Point by point he tore into the plaintiff's declaration: *The defendant has called Dr. Rush a vain boaster,* he wrote. *I aver this to be true, and prove it by Rush's own publications respecting his practice in 1793.* He cited letter after letter published during the epidemic in which the doctor had claimed his discovery reduced the fever to the danger level of the common cold. Yet mortality rates then were climbing, and just after Rush said he was curing ninety-nine out of one hundred patients, four out of five patients ill in his own house died. And again: *The defendant called Dr. Rush a quack.* What was a quack? Rush's own lawyers
220

had given the definition as a boastful pretender to phys-ick, one who proclaims his own medical ability in public places. Exactly what Rush did, Cobbett said, quoting from the newspaper notice that advised Philadelphians, with complete disregard for other physicians, how to use his cure for themselves inasmuch as he could not meet all the calls requested of him. Deaths on the day before that advertisement came to twenty-three in the city, Cobbett pointed out, but after that notice they increased to one hundred and nineteen daily. He reproduced apothecaries' ads for "DR. RUSH'S mercurial sweating powder." Would not a stranger in town have believed from the wording of that ad that Dr. Rush was a quack?

He went on to compare Rush and Dr. Sangrado of *Gil Blas* fame. He listed extracts from the novel side by side with extracts from Rush's own books. The resulting evidence was singularly devastating:

### Doctor Sangrado

"Sangrado sent me for a surgeon, whom he ordered to take from my master six good porringers of blood! When this was done he ordered the surgeon to return in three hours, and take as much more, and to repeat the same evacuation the next day!"

" 'This bleeding,' Sangrado said, 'was to supply the want of perspiration. . . .' "

"Sangrado said, 'It is a gross error, Master Martin Onez, to think that blood is necessary for the

### Doctor Rush

"I bled my patients twice, and a few three times a day. I preferred frequent and small to large bleedings in the beginning of September; but toward the height and close of the epidemic I saw no inconvenience from the loss of a pint, and even twenty ounces at one time."

"From the influence of early purging and bleeding in promoting sweat in the yellow fever, there can be little doubt but the efforts of Nature to unload the system in the plague through the pores might be accelerated by the use of the same remedies. . . ."

"You should bleed your patient almost to death, at least to fainting." This is an extract which

221

| *Doctor Sangrado* (cont.) | *Dr. Rush* (cont.) |
|---|---|
| preservation of life: a patient cannot be blooded too much.' " | Rush gives from a letter of poor old Shippen and calls it "the triumph of Reason over the formality of medicine." |
| " 'No, my friend,' Dr. Sangrado said, 'all that is required is to bleed the patients and make them drink warm water. This is the secret of curing all the distempers incident to man. Yes! that wonderful secret which Nature, impenetrable to my brethren, hath not been able to hide from my researches, is contained in these two points, of plentiful bleeding and frequent draughts of water. I have nothing more to impart; thou knowest physick to the very bottom.' " | "We teach a hundred things in our schools less useful, and many things more difficult, than the knowledge that would be necessary to cure a yellow fever or the plague. . . . A new order of things is rising in medicine as well as in government. The time must and will come when the general use of calomel, jalap, and the lancet shall be considered among the most essential articles of the knowledge and rights to man." |
| " 'I have published a book,' said Sangrado, 'in which I have extolled the use of bleeding, and would you have me decry my own book?' 'Oh no!' replied I, 'you must not give your enemies such a triumph over you. It would ruin your reputation. Perish rather the nobility, clergy, and people!' " | Rush has also published a book, and in that book he has said: "I was part of a little circle of physicians who had associated themselves in support of the new remedies. This circle would have been broken by my quitting the city. Under those circumstances it pleased God to enable me to reply to one of the letters that urged my retreat from the city, that I had resolved to stick to my principles, my practice, and my patients, to the last extremity!" |

Now, Cobbett cried hypothetically to the jury, what of the resemblance? Dr. Sangrado in the novel was called the Hippocrates of Spain, Rush by his lawyers the Hippocrates of Pennsylvania. The only difference between them was that the American gave mercury and jalap, the Spaniard warm water. The latter, Cobbett said, must be at least as innocent as the former. Gentlemen of the jury, he exclaimed, was not the name Sangrado fairly applicable to the plaintiff?

He discussed the charge that the defendant called Rush a murderer. Shameful perversion of the truth, an impudent lie, Cobbett said of the charge. He analyzed the argument of the plaintiff's counsel, and the charge itself. Had Dr. Rush been accused of killing people with deadly weapons? No, no; had the jury read the words "The Rushites have slain their tens of thousands" in a foreign newspaper they would have concluded that the doctor with his disciples followed a bold and dangerous system of medicine, but nothing more. They might have considered the doctor deceived and ignorant, but not a *criminal*. Beyond all, the passage in *Porcupine's Gazette* was in general terms, not so specific as to state *who* might have been, slain, or precisely *how,* and therefore it was not legally actionable.

Cobbett as his own lawyer made other specific points. For one, referring to the allegation that the defendant had attacked Rush because of political opinions expressed in the Rittenhouse eulogium, he pointed out that he had already disposed of that subject in *Porcupine's Gazette* long before the yellow fever ever occurred. In fact, he had attacked the eulogium in January, 1797, immediately after it was delivered. In March, 1797, he referred to it again in the "Last Will and Testament of Peter Porcupine." Long before the publication against Rush in September, the silly eulogium had been forgotten, Cobbett claimed. Therefore, the charge of malice built on this reason must disappear.

It had been said that Dr. Dewees of the Rush school was employed as a physician in Mr. Cobbett's own family. Conclusions were made that therefore the defendant was not averse to Rush's *system,* but rather to Rush himself. This impudent assertion was denied by the very fact that,

223

having carefully avoided the *system*, Cobbett was still alive. Dr. Dewees' only employment had been as obstetrician for the birth of a child, and that only by necessity for no other doctor had been available. At the time a doctor was needed, the Cobbett family resided in Bustleton outside of Philadelphia and the Cobbetts' regular doctor was in New Jersey. The implication that Dewees had been the regular family doctor was perjury.

Every one of the jury knew that when yellow fever struck in the Cobbett family—he himself had a light case and so did one of his children—his physicians were not of the "Sangrado school." One of them indeed had been the very Dr. Stevens whom Rush accused of "slaying more than the sword," and to whom the defendant along with hundreds of others owed the preservation of their lives. What better proof of Cobbett's sincerity could be had?

Cobbett closed his own defense by disdaining "hackneyed invocations to the liberty of the press." The defendant stood in need of no imaginary goddess, he sought no shelter from newly discovered principles and newfangled institutions. He begged not for mercy, but demanded justice. He reminded those who had testified against him that "He who has said, *Thou shalt not bear false witness against thy neighbor* would not be put off with subterfuges and false witnesses." He told the jury there was a final Tribunal before which they would appear not to judge but to be judged. The Searcher of all hearts, Cobbett exclaimed, in whose awful Name they had promised to do justice, would not ask whether the plaintiff were a Briton and a royalist. "The only question put to you will be: *Have you acted according to your Consciences?*"

So Cobbett concluded the defense of himself for the benefit of those concerned in the trial, for Philadelphians and for all the world who would read. Later he heard a

224

rumor that some jurors declared that if his lawyers had pleaded his case as well as he did himself, they would not have assessed against him even a shilling damages. Paltry excuses, he scoffed. He had added nothing to what they knew already. He had merely pointed up the whole jury as a set of perjured villains.

But now as he finished writing for this third issue of the *Rushlight,* William Cobbett laid his hands beside his pen on the table. He stared for a time at the countless sheets of paper he had filled. His own self-defense—he had made it now, and he felt the deflation of his spirit. All this in reality proved nothing. It was self-gratification. To speak to the jury as if it were still sitting in the box meant nothing when its decision was already three months old. He could not change it, or resist the inexorable current that had set in against him. No matter how he carried on, no matter what he wrote to expose Pennsylvania's courts of justice, no place remained for him in America. Only another land could once again find him useful.

He heard his wife in the next room. "Nancy," he called softly.

She came at once. Nancy Cobbett would never be far from his side. She moved her hand over his bowed head. His hair was ruffled, and she smoothed it gently.

"Nancy," he said with difficulty, "I have decided we will return to England."

"To England?" Nancy gasped. "Are you sure?"

He looked up heavily. "I am defeated, Nancy. They have rejected all of it. They will have no more of William Cobbett!"

At the beginning of June, 1800, newspapers in Philadelphia carried the news that Peter Porcupine had sailed away. With his wife and two children born in America he left on the packet *Arabella* from New York. Many re-

225

gretted his departure. He himself left a final message. *When people care not two straws for each other, ceremony at parting is a mere grimace,* he wrote for the papers. *I shall spare myself the trouble of a ceremonious farewell.* But, he added, if no man had more malignant foes, no one ever had more kind, sincere, and grateful friends. Under their roofs he had spent some of the happiest hours of his life. He wished to these friends peace and happiness which he feared they would not find. To his enemies he wished no severer scourge than that they prepared for themselves and their country. *With this I depart for my native land where neither the moth of democracy nor the rust of federalism doth corrupt, and where thieves do not with impunity break through and steal five thousand dollars at a time.*

## 31 *"The Most Terrible of Human Tongues"*

THE continuing story of William Cobbett reveals a curving circle of circumstance fully as amazing as the man himself.

He returned to England in that year 1800 a Tory, a firm adherent to his idealized British government. He came back to his native land with dreams of green countryside and sunny skies, with stars in his eyes about the unmatched English way of life. While blasting American democracy he had extolled Britain's monarchy so convincingly that he himself believed it was without fault.

His illusions broke apart slowly. The foundations of his faith were solid, and it took years of erosion to wear them down. He never did lose any of his faith in England itself. Cobbett remained as English as the cliffs of Dover.

Probably he himself never changed at all, but the men and the principles which he upheld became different. Or, more probably, even those principles had not really changed, for the British Government had been corrupt from the top for a long, long time, as John Wilkes knew in his day. Cobbett had merely been wrong in his misplaced judgment.

On his homecoming the Tory government received him with warmest regard. Cobbett's achievement in America on behalf of Britain made him well known and particularly welcome to the governing cliques. The conflicts of John Wilkes' time remained unsettled. The quarrels between Tories and Whigs were just as ineffectual, while a radical element representing the lower classes became more powerful. The government needed a new voice to bolster their prerogatives of power.

The returning writer began an English publication, after one false start, named the *Political Register*. He had the financial cooperation of some of the leading men in politics. He bought a farm and settled down with his family, at the age of thirty-seven, to the prospect of a reasonably ordered life. He expected to write on political subjects, and he retained a freedom of action understood even by his supporters. No one guessed the violence of the coming storm.

Cobbett soon discovered that Great Britain was shot through with oppression, discontent, political antagonism beside which America was an Eden. The beginnings of the Industrial Revolution were hitting the country with seemingly insuperable economic problems. A financial squeeze beset farmers—and Cobbett was by avocation a farmer.

He began to make suggestions for the improvement of conditions. To his surprise the simplest recommendations were received with grim silence. When Cobbett saw something he thought wrong, he had to write about it.

227

He began attacking political dogmas, then individuals in highest authority. Englishmen read, and thought. For the second time William Cobbett grew to be a major factor over popular opinion throughout a whole nation. But *this* time the government itself turned out to be his opposition.

The crisis came with a case where British soldiers were flogged by German mercenaries after a minor mutiny over supplies. Englishmen whipped by foreigners! Cobbett burst forth in a blaze of indignation against the affair, and roared at government policies which could allow such a thing to happen. He did not spare officials responsible. He had been a soldier himself. Alone, the incident was unimportant enough, but to the already nettled British Government it was an opportunity. Because of it, Cobbett went to Newgate Prison for two years on a charge of sedition.

Here was an odd repetition of John Wilkes' imprisonment of years before. Cobbett, too, had his own apartment in jail, his friends and family to stay with him, his adequate food supply. During his term he continued to write and publish his *Register*. By putting William Cobbett in prison, the government made a fearful mistake which they did not realize at the time, for they turned him into a force that after his release shook the roots of the Empire.

The development of Cobbett was slow but sure. He became finally the spokesman against tyranny over lower classes, new industrial workers, the farmers, the poor. Spokesman? He was a trumpet, an organ thundering for justice for the common man. His written words brought down leaders of the government, changed laws, and before the end advanced by years the great Reform which carried England into its modern era.

Strange that for half his lifetime Cobbett fought for the same elements of liberty for which Thomas Jefferson stood—strange that it took so long for him to recognize what he may have believed the whole time. But he never thought of himself as a *republican*—always as a royalist. Except that the royalist government must be, in his opinion, a government fairly for the people, all the people.

He acknowledged a change of heart about one of his old adversaries, another Englishman. This was Thomas Paine, of whom Peter Porcupine had written so bitterly in the Philadelphia days. Cobbett made a return trip to America in 1817. He came to escape the possibility of a second British jail sentence. He rented a farm near Hempstead, Long Island, and continued writing from this distance for English publication. He kept clear of American politics, but did report to the English people with enthusiasm on the freedom of American life. It was a remarkable difference in attitudes. Cobbett had opened his eyes wide.

During his stay he discovered that Thomas Paine was buried in New Rochelle, above New York City. Paine, because of his deist and anti-clerical writings, had been denied Christian burial by any denomination. Cobbett, as an act of atonement for Porcupine's attacks, received permission to disinter Paine from the unhallowed ground. He conceived the noteworthy idea that Paine must be buried in his native England with honors Cobbett believed due, and a monument should be erected to his memory.

Cobbett took Paine's bones with him back across the Atlantic. A certain amount of trouble arose when the coffin was presented to the English customs authorities. Having settled that difficulty, Cobbett discovered that his good intention was received with hilarity and ridicule throughout England. The political implications were not lost by his opponents. Even Lord Byron, no enemy of Cobbett, took the occasion for a sly bit of humor:

229

In digging up your bones, Tom Paine,
Will Cobbett has done well;
You'll visit him on earth again,
He'll visit you in Hell.

But Cobbett found cold response on all sides to his suggestion that a decent burial and a memorial should be provided for a fellow Englishman. As a result, Cobbett kept in his possession for the rest of his life the coffin and the bones. He left them to his son, who found in later bankruptcy that Thomas Paine was no financial asset. It seems that many of the bones finally disappeared in a secondhand dealer's shop, although decades later some of them were recovered for more dignified disposal.

Thomas Paine, John Wilkes—among so many others including the greatest of all, Thomas Jefferson—were essentially leaders of revolutions for the liberty of the ordinary man. William Cobbett came to reach a high rank in their company.

The Rush lawsuit in Philadelphia had one serious twist in Cobbett's later life. When he was on trial in England for his seditious writing he defended himself. His self-defense on that occasion turned out to be particularly inadequate, and he was convicted. But again later, this time in his sixty-ninth year, he stood on trial before Parliament charged with inciting riots against the government. Once more he spoke in his own defense, and so brilliantly that he turned the case against himself into a smashing indictment of conditions which permitted the riots to occur.

William Cobbett died in 1835, aged seventy-two, and a member of Parliament. He was survived by his wife Nancy and seven children. Gilbert K. Chesterton wrote a graphic description of the big, stubborn, self-educated

230

man who shook two nations with his writing. It provides a most fitting eulogy:

"Certainly if they put him in prison, they ought never to have let him out. . . . The man who came out of that prison was not the man who went in. It is not enough to say that he came out in a rage, and may be said to have remained in a rage; to have lived in a rage for thirty years, until he died in a rage in his own place upon the hills of Surrey. There are rages and rages; and they ought to have seen in his eyes when they opened the door that they had let loose a revolution. We talk of a man being in a towering passion; and that vigorous phrase, so much in his own literary manner, is symbolic of his intellectual importance. He did indeed return in a towering passion, a passion that towered above towns and villages like a waterspout, or a cyclone visible from ten counties and crossing England like the stride of the storm. The most terrible of human tongues was loosened and went through the country like a wandering bell, of incessant anger and alarum; till men must have wondered why, when it was in their power, they had not cut it out."

## 32 "— Not Another Person Who Can Die--"

SHAPES of men called great rise slowly out of the murky swirl of their own times. Their profiles emerge first, then heads and shoulders until at last the full figures stand forth for the world's respect. So it was with Benjamin Rush.

In the city of Philadelphia the name of Peter Porcupine disappeared into the recesses of people's memories.

In the first year of the new century the Federal government moved to Washington. Yellow fever appeared from time to time again, but never with the violence of the previous decade. Medical controversies about bleeding and purging became a part of Philadelphia's colorful history.

Dr. Benjamin Rush attended to his patients and applied himself to his studies. He had kept silent while the remainder of the *Rushlights* were circulating. And, after a time, the lawsuit judgment was finally paid.

In the course of a few months, Rush himself said, the persecutions against him were neglected and forgotten. He quoted the truth of a remark he had often heard from his old friend Dr. Witherspoon, that: *Scandal dies sooner of itself than we could kill it.*

After the year 1800 Dr. Rush came to be recognized as the leading physician in America. A clique of other doctors retained a scornful disdain for him, but nevertheless he reached an importance in his own right equivalent to the one-time reputation of Dr. Cullen of Edinburgh. Rush was the great preceptor and teacher, using his post at the University of Pennsylvania to pass on his system to eager pupils. Benjamin Rush was responsible for the medical education of more than three thousand physicians. They carried the practice of his theories to every part of the United States.

His books were read and followed not only by the American profession but also in foreign lands. He was admired, respected throughout the British Empire and Europe. Dr. Rush was one of the first men to prove to the world that America could produce a high level of learning and intelligence. His stature in foreign eyes at that time nearly equaled the giant fame of Franklin. Not many other Americans ever achieved equivalent contemporary renown.

The energetic physician of Philadelphia rose above

the storms of criticism and attacks of his middle years to rare greatness toward the end of his own lifetime. As he drove about the streets of his city, the townspeople recognized him and knew him as one of their notable assets.

After the Cobbett affair, Rush wrote his autobiography. He intended it particularly as a self-defense of his own for the benefit of his children and descendants, after the many controversies which his character endured. But the autobiography records a brilliant and revealing history of the American Revolution and the personalities concerned in it. Taken together with his Commonplace Books—random daily notes—and with his published letters, Benjamin Rush's writings are a memorable landmark of early American literature.

Rush himself put on record the final end of the William Shippen feud. In 1808 Dr. Shippen lay dying, alone, and after years of tragic family events. He called in Rush at long last, professionally. There was nothing Rush could do, but the quarrel ended. "He was my enemy," Rush noted. With a supreme spirit of forgiveness he said that he attended the doctor with "a sincere desire to prolong his life. Peace and joy to his soul forever and forever."

Many of Dr. Rush's medical opinions crumpled under later scientific research. Bloodletting, salivation, intense purging gave way in the treatment of most diseases to newer discoveries. But, wrong though he was in many respects, his place as the first American physician to cast out old theories and adopt new ones can never be usurped.

In one field of medicine Rush has stood solidly until this day. He can be classed as the first true American psychiatrist. He lived long enough to complete the greatest monument to his life. In 1812 Benjamin Rush published his book on *Medical Inquiries and Observations upon the Diseases of the Mind*.

The book was not well received at first by Philadelphia's medical men. The subject was too new for them to understand. In other places the volume was appreciated quickly. Its fame and value grew with deeper realization of the subject itself. Before long Benjamin Rush's *Observations upon the Diseases of the Mind* achieved the status of not only the best but the only textbook of its kind available.

Translated into foreign languages and used by doctors and students everywhere, the book remained a standard authority for seventy years.

Dr. Rush made the point that mental ills were caused by diseases of the brain, just as diseases of other tissues caused physical ills. Insanity primarily originated in the brain's blood vessels, but also extended to the nerves. He proved his conclusions by autopsies. He inquired into the unexplored areas of the mind itself, figuratively speaking, as no one in America had before. He developed causes of derangement, some from injuries and disorders in the brain, others from physical shock to the brain or the whole body. But mental shock caused derangement, too, he stated, even more commonly. He analyzed causes, for the most part with modern accuracy: guilt, loneliness, fear, excessive anger. Climate, he felt, was a factor. Heredity was a cause.

He recommended shock treatments with his hot and cold bath applications. And Rush anticipated without fully realizing why the basic treatment of modern psychiatry. Hire a companion for mad patients, he urged the trustees of the Pennsylvania Hospital. Let such a companion talk to the ill ones sympathetically so they would confide their troubles. He told the physicians to listen to patients' stories. He himself often asked deranged persons to write about themselves on paper. They felt better afterward, and Rush learned much about them that was helpful to his treatment.

234

Rush discovered what Freud so long later identified: relief of the subconscious through self-expression.

For years Dr. Rush and his long-time friend John Adams, living at Quincy, Massachusetts, kept up an intimate and fascinating correspondence with each other, reviewing political and philosophical as well as personal affairs throughout their eventful lives. Rush managed at last to bring Thomas Jefferson into a letter-writing triangle. Jefferson and Adams had quarreled long before over differences of political opinions. Rush reconciled them, all by letter, with diplomatic adroitness. It was a remarkable trio of Americans corresponding with one another.

On the tenth of April, 1813, Rush wrote a letter to John Adams. As usual he ranged over a variety of subjects. He mentioned the rise of the American Navy, and a victory at sea over the British. The War of 1812 was continuing. His son Ben had arrived safely home from Smyrna, having escaped pirates and British cruisers.

Four days later Dr. Rush visited his usual number of patients, attended to his numerous duties. That night he had a chill, aggravating a cough which had bothered him for years. Fever developed, and in the morning the doctor had himself bled ten ounces.

Typhus, said the doctor called in to attend him. Pulmonary tuberculosis, Rush contradicted him. He knew this to be the end. He told his son James, who had returned from Edinburgh as an M.D. After five days of illness, tranquilly and without fear, Benjamin Rush died on the nineteenth of April, 1813.

He died as a notable American. The verdict of the jury in 1799 had been well sustained.

Philadelphians mourned. Eulogies flowed in from across the land, from across the seas. But the tributes that came from Dr. Rush's two closest friends, both of them former presidents of the United States, best defined the character and life of the Philadelphia physician.

Thomas Jefferson wrote to John Adams: *Another of our friends of '76 is gone, my dear sir, and another of the co-signers of the Independence of our country. And a better man than Rush could not have left us, more benevolent, more learned, of finer genius, or more honest.*

And John Adams said of his friend: *As a man of science, letters, taste, sense, philosophy, patriotism, religion, morality, merit, usefulness, taken altogether, Rush has not left his equal in America; nor that I know of in the world.*

Then Adams wrote to Richard Rush in a deeply felt letter of sorrow, *In what terms can I address you? There are none that can express my sympathy with you and your family, or my own personal feelings on the loss of your excellent father. There is not another person, out of my own family, who can die in whom my personal happiness can be so deeply affected.* He added with Yankee dryness *—The world would pronounce me extravagant and no man would apologize for me if I should say that in the estimation of unprejudiced philosophy, he had done more good in this world than Franklin or Washington.*

# Bibliography

## CONTEMPORARY SOURCES:

Adams, Abigail. *New Letters of Abigail Adams.* Stewart Mitchell, ed. (Houghton Mifflin Co.: Boston, 1947).

Adams, John. *The Works of John Adams.* C. F. Adams, ed., 10 vols. (Little, Brown & Co.: Boston, 1850—1856).

Carey, Mathew. *A Short Account of the Malignant Fever, Lately Prevalent in Philadelphia* . . . 3rd ed., improved (Philadelphia, 1793).

Cobbett, William. *Advice to Young Men and Incidentally to Young Women* . . . (London, n.d.).

————. *Letters from William Cobbett to Edward Thornton Written in the Years, 1797 to 1800.* G. D. H. Cole, ed. (Oxford University Press: London, 1939).

————. *Life and Adventures of Peter Porcupine* (Philadelphia, 1796).

————. *The Life and Letters of William Cobbett in England and America Based upon Hitherto Unpublished Papers,* by Lewis Melville, 2 vols. (John Lane: London, 1913).

————. *The Life of William Cobbett Dedicated to His Sons* (Carey & Hart: Philadelphia, 1835).

————. *Political Censor, 1796—1797.* Philadelphia.

————. *Political Register* (1804, 1805, 1820, 1829, Philadelphia).

————. *Porcupine's Works* . . . , 12 vols. (London, 1801).

————. *A Year's Residence in the United States* (London, 1822).

Condie, Thomas and Richard Folwell. *History of the Pestilence, Commonly Called Yellow Fever* . . . (Philadelphia, 1798).

Cutler, W. C. and J. P. *Life, Journals and Correspondence of Rev. Manesseh Cutler* (Robert Clarke & Co.: Cincinnati, 1888).

Folwell, Richard. *A Short History of the Yellow Fever* . . . , *Philadelphia July 1797,* 2nd ed. (Philadelphia, 1798).

Hamilton, Alexander. *The Works of Alexander Hamilton.* Henry Cabot Lodge, ed., 12 vols. (G. P. Putnam & Sons: New York, 1904).

237

Hamilton, Alexander. *The Works of Alexander Hamilton, Comprising His Correspondence and His Political and Official Writings* . . . John C. Hamilton, ed., 7 vols. (C. S. Francis & Co.: New York, 1851).

Jefferson, Thomas. *The Writings of Thomas Jefferson.* A. A. Liscomb and A. L. Bergh, 20 vols. (T. Jefferson Memorial Asso.: Washington, 1903).

Paine, Thomas. *Writings of Thomas Paine.* M. D. Conway, ed., 4 vols. (G. P. Putnam & Sons: New York, 1895).

Pennsylvania Hospital, *Records. Managers' Report, 1799.* In Pennsylvania Hospital archives.

Philadelphia Library, Ridgeway Branch. Manuscript Collection. This branch, founded by James Rush, son of Benjamin Rush, has a large collection of Rush papers and documents.

Ramsay, David. *An Eulogium upon Benjamin Rush, M.D.* (Bradford & Inskeep: Philadelphia, 1813).

*A Report of an Action for a Libel, Brought by Dr. Benjamin Rush Against William Cobbett, In the Supreme Court of Pennsylvania, December Term, 1799* . . . Recorded by T. Carpenter, Court Stenographer (Philadelphia, 1800).

Rush, Benjamin. *An Account of the Bilious Remitting Yellow Fever, as it Appeared in the City of Philadelphia, in the Year 1793* (Dobson: Philadelphia, 1794).

———. *The Autobiography of Benjamin Rush. His "Travels Through Life" Together with his "Commonplace Book" for 1789—1813.* George W. Corner, ed. (Princeton University Press: Princeton, 1948).

———. *Directions for Preserving the Health of Soldiers* (Lancaster, 1778).

———. *An Eulogium Intended to Perpetuate the Memory of David Rittenhouse, Late President of the American Philosophical Society* (Ormrod & Conrad: Philadelphia, 1796).

———. *Letters of Benjamin Rush.* L. H. Butterfield, ed., 2 vols. (Princeton University Press: Princeton, 1951).

Van Doren, Carl. *Benjamin Franklin's Autobiographical Writings* (The Viking Press: New York, 1945).

Washington, George. *The Writings of George Washington from the Original Manuscript Sources, 1745—1799.* John C. Fitzpatrick, ed., 39 vols. (U.S. Government Printing Office: Washington, 1937).

———. *The Writings of George Washington* . . . Jared Sparks, ed. (American Stationers' Co.: Boston, 1834).

Watson, J. F. *Annals of Philadelphia and Pennsylvania in the Olden Time* (Whiting & Thomas: Philadelphia, 1857).

## NEWSPAPERS:

*Aurora.* Philadelphia, 1794—1829.
*Claypoole's American Daily Advertiser.* Philadelphia, 1799.
*Dunlap's American Daily Advertiser.* Philadelphia, 1793.
*Gazette of the United States and Philadelphia Daily Advertiser.* Philadelphia, 1799.
*Pennsylvania Gazette.* Philadelphia, 1799.
*Philadelphia Gazette and Universal Daily Advertiser.* Philadelphia, 1799.
*Porcupine's Gazette.* Philadelphia, 1797.

## SECONDARY WORKS:

Bleackley, Horace. *Life of John Wilkes* (J. Lane: London, 1917).
Bowen, Marjorie. *Peter Porcupine. A Study of William Cobbett, 1762—1835* (Longmans, Green & Co.: New York, 1935).
Bronson, W. W., and Charles Hildebrand. *Inscriptions in St. Peter's Church Yard* (Camden, 1897).
Butterfield, L. H. "Love and Valor; or Benjamin Rush and the Leslies of Edinburgh," *Princeton University Library Chronicle,* IX (1947—1948).
Chesterton, G. K. *William Cobbett* (Dodd, Mead Co.: New York, 1926).
Clark, Mary Elizabeth. *Peter Porcupine in America: The Career of William Cobbett, 1792—1800* (Times & News: Philadelphia, 1939).
Cole, G. D. H. *The Life of William Cobbett* (W. Collins Sons & Co.: London, 1924).
Dutton, W. F. *Venesection* (F. A. Davis: Philadelphia, 1916).
Earle, Alice Morse. *Two Centuries of Costume in America* (Macmillan: New York, 1903).
*Encyclopedia Britannica,* 14th ed., 1940.
Flexner, J. T. *Doctors on Horseback, Pioneers of American Medicine* (Viking Press: New York, 1937).
Goodman, Nathan G. *Benjamin Rush, Physician and Citizen* (University of Pennsylvania: Philadelphia, 1934).
Konkle, Burton Alva. *Joseph Hopkinson, 1770—1842* . . . (University of Pennsylvania: Philadelphia, 1931).

239

Major, Ralph H. *A History of Medicine,* 2 vols. (Thomas: Springfield, Ill., 1954).

McClellan, Elizabeth. *Historic Dress in America, 1607—1800* (G. W. Jacobs & Co.: Philadelphia, 1917).

Morais, Henry S. *Jews of Philadelphia* (Levytype Co.: Philadelphia, 1894).

Morris, Richard B. *Encyclopedia of American History* (Harper: New York, 1953).

Morse, John T. *John Adams* (Houghton, Mifflin & Co.: Boston, 1908).

Norris, George W. *The Early History of Medicine in Philadelphia* (Collins: Philadelphia, 1886).

Osler, Sir William. *The Evolution of Modern Medicine* (New Haven, 1922).

Pepper, O. H. Perry. "Benjamin Rush's Theories on Bloodletting After 150 Years," *Transactions and Studies, College of Physicians, Philadelphia,* XIV, December, 1946.

Powell, John H. *Bring Out Your Dead* (University of Pennsylvania: Philadelphia, 1949).

Scharf, J. T. and Thompson Westcott. *History of Philadelphia, 1609—1884,* 3 vols. (L. H. Everts & Co.: Philadelphia, 1884).

Thompson, C. J. S. *History of Surgical Instruments* (Schuman: New York, 1942).

*Universal Jewish Encyclopedia.*

Van Doren, Carl. *Benjamin Franklin* (Viking Press: New York, 1938).

Wardrop, James. *On Bloodletting* (J. B. Baillière: London, 1835).

Warren, Charles. *A History of the American Bar* (Little, Brown & Co.: Boston, 1911).

240

# Index

242

243

244

10 & 10 (medicine): see Purging
Tilghman, Edward, 163, 185-187, 201
Tilton, Dr. James, 134-135, 137
Trial, the, 4-9, 12, 17, 19, 20-25, 132, 140, 151-152, 155, 159-196, 200, 206, 208, 213, 217, 219, 230, 232; *charge to jury,* 192-195; *jury,* 18-19, 21-23, 25, 159, 162, 164, 171, 174, 179, 181-182, 184-185, 187, 191, 194-195, 209, 215, 219, 225; *verdict,* 195-196, 200, 207, 235

*United States Gazette, The,* 111, 131, 133, 135
University of Pennsylvania: see Pennsylvania, University of

Venesection: see Bleeding
Verdict, jury's, 195-196, 200, 207, 235. See also Trial

Wallace, Rebecca (BR's sister), 34-37, 43, 56, 58, 81-84, 89
War of Independence, 8, 11-12, 14, 17-18, 30, 48, 51, 62, 68, 76, 107, 111, 114, 121-122, 145, 218, 233

Washington, George, 4, 17, 51, 76-77, 88, 99, 107, 113-116, 122-124, 153, 178, 207, 216, 218, 236
Way, Dr. Nicholas, 130-131
Webster, Noah, 109
Wilkes, John, 15-16, 101, 227-228, 230
Wistar, Dr. Caspar, 48, 57, 65-66, 75, 119
Witherspoon, Rev. Dr. John, 40, 232

X Y Z Affair, 4, 152

Yates, Jasper, 19, 23
Yellow fever, 120, 166-168, 171, 192, 224, 232; *epidemic 1793,* 7, 24-25, 29-38, 41-50, 55-58, 61-82, 84, 86-88, 97-98, 119, 128, 141, 161, 172, 185-186, 212, 220-221; *epidemic 1797,* 9, 126-130, 132, 135-136, 138-139, 172, 181, 187, 209, 220, 223
Young, Dr. Thomas, 62-63
Yrujo, Chevalier Charles de, 148-149